African Literature and the Future

This book is a product of the CODESRIA 13th General Assembly, 2011

Africa and the Challenges of the Twenty-first Century

African Literature and the Future

Edited by

Gbemisola Adeoti

Council for the Development of Social Science Research in Africa
DAKAR

Council for the Development of Social Science Research in Africa
Avenue Cheikh Anta Diop, Angle Canal IV
BP 3304 Dakar, 18524, Senegal
Website : www.codesria.org
ISBN : 978-2-86978-633-2

Typesetting: Alpha Ousmane Dia
Cover Design: Ibrahima Fofana

Distributed in Africa by CODESRIA
Distributed elsewhere by African Books Collective, Oxford, UK
Website: www.africanbookscollective.com

The Council for the Development of Social Science Research in Africa (CODESRIA) is an independent organisation whose principal objectives are to facilitate research, promote research-based publishing and create multiple forums geared towards the exchange of views and information among African researchers. All these are aimed at reducing the fragmentation of research in the continent through the creation of thematic research networks that cut across linguistic and regional boundaries.

CODESRIA publishes *Africa Development*, the longest standing Africa based social science journal; *Afrika Zamani*, a journal of history; the *African Sociological Review*; the *African Journal of International Affairs*; *Africa Review of Books* and the *Journal of Higher Education in Africa*. The Council also co-publishes the *Africa Media Review*; *Identity, Culture and Politics: An Afro-Asian Dialogue*; *The African Anthropologist* and the *Afro-Arab Selections for Social Sciences*. The results of its research and other activities are also disseminated through its Working Paper Series, Green Book Series, Monograph Series, Book Series, Policy Briefs and the CODESRIA Bulletin. Select CODESRIA publications are also accessible online at www.codesria.org.

CODESRIA would like to express its gratitude to the Swedish International Development Cooperation Agency (SIDA), the International Development Research Centre (IDRC), the Ford Foundation, the Carnegie Corporation of New York (CCNY), the Norwegian Agency for Development Cooperation (NORAD), the Danish Agency for International Development (DANIDA), the Netherlands Ministry of Foreign Affairs, the Rockefeller Foundation, the Open Society Foundations (OSFs), Trust Africa, UNESCO, UN Women, the African Capacity Building Foundation (ACBF) and the Government of Senegal for supporting its research, training and publication programmes.

Content

About the Contributors

Gbemisola Adeoti, Professor and Director, Institute of Cultural Studies, English Department, Obafemi Awolowo University, Ile Ife, Nigeria.

Henry Hunjo, Lecturer, Department of English, Lagos State University, Ojoo, Nigeria.

Olusola Ogunbayo, Lecturer, English Department of Redeemer's University, Mowe, Ogun State, Nigeria.

Stephen Ogundipe, Lecturer of poetry and African oral literature, English Department, Obafemi Awolowo University, Ile Ife, Nigeria.

Inyani Simala, Lecturer, Department of Language and Literature Education, Masinde Muliro University of Science and Technology, Kakamega, Kenya.

Sule E. Egya, Senior Lecturer, English Department, Ibrahim Badamasi Babangida University, Lapai, Niger State, Nigeria.

Introduction

Present Tension in Future Tenses: Re-writing Africa into the Twenty-first Century

Gbemisola Adeoti

The tale of Africa's march through the labyrinth of history is long and multilayered. If can, however be aptly summarised through the framework of paradox and irony. From ancient times to the period of slavery and colonialism to the present era of neo-colonialism, the continent and its people are defined by simultaneous visibility and absence, excitement and neglect, power and powerlessness. Did the African monarchs not wield so much power over their people? But were those powers not appropriated by the colonialists in a way that made the native rulers mere spectators in the arena of their own dance? The post-independence states are supposed to be sovereign, but the levers of economic and political control reside in the donor states (USA, Britain, France, Netherlands, Germany and so on), thus, creating a situation of freedom cut short by debilitating dependence.

It is within these interstices of irony and paradox that we can probe the harsh reality of mass poverty amidst opulence of the few; joblessness amidst apparent growth in services and other neglected sectors; and unending violence in spite of huge investment in security. Not in many fora is this complex reality that defines Africa more trenchantly articulated than in imaginative literature produced about and on the continent. This is the crux of the six essays collected in this book.

In the decades of the 1950s and 1960s, many African countries attained what was described as 'independence' from colonial rule. The wave of independence that swept through a substantial part of Africa was salutary, imbuing the people with great expectations. Independence struggles created much hope for freedom from domination by foreign rulers who seized the continent and turned the owners of the homestead into squatters on their own soil. But as the sun was setting on the empire, so it seemed, the colonies were wearing a new badge of repression, this time, from their own kinsmen.

The euphoria soon dried up. The gleeful songs of *uhuru* were drowned by martial music and songs of war amidst political turmoil from nation to nation. Many of the crises in the 1960s which still persist in some African countries today were generated by the 'looser-looses-all' type of politics that saw political contest as war and the resultant power which it conferred as a door to endless booties. Consequently, democratic spaces were shrinking where the ruling party frazzled opposition parties out of existence or soldiers brazenly dismantled democratic structures under martial rule.

Another sore point was the deepening and entrenchment of racist rule in South Africa, Angola, Mozambique, Namibia, Zimbabwe and Zambia. The relentless onslaught against racist regimes in these countries yielded fruits with the gradual collapse of minority rule and enthronement of black majority rule, the most memorable being the victory of the African National Congress led by Nelson Mandela in the 1994 election in South Africa. This was after the independence of Angola, Mozambique and Zimbabwe.

However, some pertinent questions arise: how has Africa fared five decades after independence? What dividend have the nations derived from their supposed political freedom? How fulfilled is the hope of political liberation and economic development? How united and integrated are the diverse people and culture of the continent? Are poverty, disease and ignorance banished from the land as promised by the nationalists and successive politicians?

From the available indices, living conditions in many African countries are still harsh and bleak. True liberation is as elusive as economic prosperity while political stability remains a mirage in the vortex of ethno-religious violence and communal crisis.

Over a decade into the new millennium, the much advertised Millennium Development Goals remain at the level of vain hopes and empty propositions in many communities in Africa. Rising insurgency is gnawing at the heart of the continent, threatening its future in the Twenty-first century.

The need to reflect on Africa's past and present to address anxieties about the future through the epistemological lens of literature is the driving force of this collection of essays. Here, literature provides the broad canvass through which the six authors interrogate Africa's past and speculate about the possibilities that lie ahead in the future. The authors approach, from different perspectives, the trend and tenor of politics and their impacts on the socio-cultural and economic development of the continent as portrayed in imaginative writings over the years The exercise can, therefore, be summed up as 'peeping ahead from a backward glance'.

To re-emphasise, literature is one of the knowledge tools designed by man from ancient times to dissect and straighten the crooked ribs of a society. In its oral, written, performative, narrative, poetic or screen-mediated forms, literature speaks to the people, and confronts the dynamics of history. It is a vintage observatory from where the writer is strategically placed to observe the goings-on in the society. He may distort or realistically re-present the picture to create awareness and effect changes where necessary for social transformation. In the process, the goal of entertainment is achieved.

One salient feature of African literature is the close affinity between art and politics in its polemics. This is well established in all the six essays in the book. The authors stress the interconnections between literature and society in the critical analyses of the texts that they engage. From the tone of their analyses, there is an overwhelming feeling of angst and pessimism, but the authors recognise a flicker hope in spite of daunting odds, given certain conditions. Thus, they depict the plausible fate of Africa in the Twenty-first century, as informed by its ancient and recent past, gleaned from primary texts. They also address the aesthetic forms that shape the writers' various philosophical and ideological responses to socio-historical realities.

Of central concern to writers and critics of African literature is the predicament of a continent bogged down by the frustration of the ideals of independence for which the nationalists struggled. Like Soyinka, Armah, Ngugi, Awoonor, Osundare, Okri and many other African writers, the critics here contend that the absence of genuine democracy has negatively impacted on the economy of many African countries over the years. This has widened the gap between rich and poor. Writers have not only decried this harsh reality in their various works, some have proceeded to prescribe alternative routes out of what Soyinka is wont to describe as an unending 'season of anomy'. Thus, realising the limitations of art for art's sake, the writers constantly engage society and its problems. There is a close link between developments in African political history and thematic concerns of literary productions; whether in the caustic satires of Soyinka or in the pro-Marxist aesthetics of Sembène Ousmane, Ngugi wa Thiong'o and Festus Iyayi, or in the return-to-roots ideas of Armah, p'Bitek and Okri.

Another feature of African literature is its dual heritage which is expressed from writer to writer in the fusion of traditional oral resources with influences derived from classics in Western literature, to which African writers were exposed in the course of their education. As part of the traditional sources, African writers draw from myth, folklore, legend, festivals and ritual performances. Thus, they use artistic conventions derived from the dual heritage to articulate their thematic concerns.

Contemporary African writers, like those of other societies, have recognised the 'transforming and reforming potentials of literature'. They are social critics who dissect the present, and seers who project into the future. The writer as an artist is believed to be endowed with an extra-sensory perception; a keen eye for observing social events; a critical consciousness for interpreting these events and an aesthetic orientation for processing them into a recognisable artistic genre. Hence, the writer is somehow a step ahead of his time and society in apprehending reality. African writers produce the kind of literature that Niyi Osundare has in mind when he writes:

> The call at the moment seems to be one for a literature of praxis, a concrete activist literature with a clamorous statement about the social situation. This call is most persistent among third world writers, representatives of people for so long victims of capitalist exploitation and imperialism (2007: 10).

As Osundare remarks further, social issue 'is not an aside, but the very heart of creative consciousness, meant to change the world in the process' (2007: 30). This enduring social commitment of literature, even from its mythical antecedents, is well acknowledged in all the essays in this collection, starting from Inyani Simala's 'Orality, Modernity and African Development: Myth as Dialogue of Civilisation'. While advancing a universal and timeless theory of myth, Simala notes that the past intrudes into the modern era and lingers on into the future through myth. Every civilisation has myths that oil its wheel of progress and sustain its march through history. As Simala submits, myth survives beyond the context of oral culture. It finds expression in modernity, and since development is a universal and an enduring desire of human societies there is the need to demythologise development which, in Western thought, is viewed from the material rather than human perspective.

An act of demythologisation as urged by Simala is in the area of the history of civilisation, an arena from which Africa is either totally absent or irreverently represented in marginal terms. Myth, from its fabulous origin, can influence the construction of a modern world that is founded on genuine advancements of humans where the pain of one is not the gain of another as typical of a capitalist order. Myth, he agrees, is often associated with the ancient past or old order, but it is a medium through which we can come to terms with and properly understand Africa and its people.

Its passage from one generation to another generation accounts for the archetypal patterns as well as the plurality of voices, multiplicity of references and cross-cultural echoes found in myth. Simala rejects the tendency to bind myth to the realm of tradition by some Western scholars who regard it as 'pre-modern' and 'anti-development'. Rather, he makes a case for a theory of myth that breaks out of the traditional epistemological vise and re-emphasises it as the engine that drives social growth and economic well-being. In that case, it is no longer the record of a still moment in history when the march of civilisation seems to be halted or frozen in motion. In his words, it is the paradigm of 'civilisations in dialogue', in a subtle reconsideration of Samuel Huntington's postulations about the 'clash of civilisations', Fukuyama's putative 'end of history' and Michel Foucault's 'theory of power'.

While dismissing the tendency to equate modernity with development as fallacious, Simala contends that a modernity which has literacy as one of its features, as against orality, is not peculiar to the West. Similarly, orality which is associated with tradition, pre-modernity and lack of development, is not a *cul de sac* in which Africa is irretrievably bound and blocked. Myth is, therefore, not peculiar to Africa and neither is civilisation or modernity the exclusive preserve of Europe as often presented in the colonialist imagination. This implies that orality is not in any way inferior to writing, just as civilisation that is emblematised in writing is not the gift of Europe to Africa.

To realise the dreams of true liberation, self-reliance, stability, democratic governance, and other ideals nursed by African nationalists as encapsulated in Nkrumah's *Consciencism*, Nyerere's *Ujamaa* (African Socialism), Kenyatta's *Harambee* and Awolowo's *People's Republic*, Simala argues that in the Twenty-first century (which in this context is taken as the signpost of the future), development should wear a more congenial human face, rather than being limited to the development of infrastructure and material production as often stressed in neo-liberal economic literature with its abiding interest in individualism, the supremacy of market forces and deification of capital. Human beings, according to Simala, should be the ultimate goal and the beneficiary of development efforts. He concludes that a materialist approach adopted hitherto, with its emphasis on reform, rolling back the state, expanding the frontiers of capital and priveleging market forces can no longer work in the Twenty-first century because it is alienating. In his words, 'no African country can develop without paying considerable attention to crucial cultural elements including myth and orality'. Thus, in place of a development that flows from the narrow prisms of technology and economic growth, he opts for a version encompassing the whole of people's life, 'integrating all the dimensions of life and all the energies of a community'. What Africa needs most at present and in its future is a synergy of culture and development towards the formulation of an alternative development model. Such a model will be rooted in indigenous culture and popular participation.

The place of the people in governance and development is the concern of Adeoti in his examination of absolute rule, its manifestations in post-independence Africa and its implications for democratisation and development as dramatised in Wole Soyinka's plays. In 'Requiem for Absolutism: Soyinka and the Re-visioning of Governance in Twenty-first Century Africa', I submit that good governance, the type that democracy offers, is a more congenial pathway to socio-economic development, compared with various forms of absolute rule – monarchy, totalitarianism, oligarchy, theocracy and so on. This is also Soyinka's position canvassed not only in the two plays analysed in my essay (*The Beatification of*

Area Boy and *King Baabu*), but also in many other creative works and public intervention discourses. Soyinka prescribes a relentless onslaught against all forms of absolute rule manifesting as one party civilian rule or military oligarchy. This necessitates constant combat with anti-democratic tendencies in a democratic order whenever apprehended.

The military has been a recurring factor in post-independence politics in Africa. Many of the countries slipped into military rule within the first decade of independence – Nigeria, Ghana, Togo, Sierra Leone, Uganda, Central African Republic. In the case of Soyinka's Nigeria, the military ruled for three decades of the first fifty years of independence. While in power, the soldiers proved to be part of the societal problems to be solved rather than being the solution. Violence, corruption, insecurity and other 'sins', of which they accuse civilian regimes, still rage on under their watch. Soyinka uses the arts of music, poetry and drama to demystify the soldiers, showing them as being incapable of nurturing democracy. The first step towards democratisation, he argues, is to keep the military out of politics. As evident from the patterns of conflict and the denouement of the two plays, Soyinka shows that no meaningful development can take place until those who attain power undemocratically, and exercise it without recourse to the people, are kept permanently out of the arena of power. Absolutism in African governance has turned many communities that have ordinarily lived together in peace for hundreds of years against each other; they are engulfed in violent conflicts. For the continent to advance in the Twenty-first century, indices of arbitrariness must be removed from the polity.

In both *The Beatification* and *King Baabu* the military is depicted as a wrong prescription and an ineffective antidote for underdevelopment. Soldiers are portrayed as another set of colonialists who pillage people's resources. This emerges more clearly in their re-creation in Guatuna Empire under the autarchy superintended by Basha Bash who later transforms into King Baabu. I call for a general psychological re-birth in the pursuit of African renaissance. This implies that both the dominating martial order and the dominated populace need to undergo psychological change so as to bring about values that can sustain democracy and energise drive for development.

Soyinka's politics as captured in his art is also the subject of Henry Hunjo's essay in the third chapter. The author examines Soyinka's autobiographical works from the perspective of critical discourse evaluation. The central concern is the possibility of true liberation from colonialism, given the nature of the postcolonial state and the character of the elite who inherit powers from the colonialists. As revealed by Hunjo, Soyinka harbours grave suspicion and distrust of many African leaders, politicians and bureaucrats who took over the reins of the state after independence. It is not surprising, therefore, that the dreams of the nationalists at independence died on arrival in some countries. Leadership, in this regard is a major factor in Africa's postcolonial predicament. As Hunjo deciphers from Soyinka's writings, the issue of leadership must be critically and holistically tackled, or meaningful development will continue to elude the continent even as the candle of the second decade of the Twenty-first century continues to burn, almost imperceptibly, but with astonishing rapidity.

Like Adeoti, Hunjo acknowledges that Soyinka's works are largely motivated by issues of politics and governance. To gain appreciable insights into his art, one needs to be abreast of political (under)currents in Africa. Admittedly, Soyinka has been accused of nursing a pessimistic view of Africa's history as he contends that the promises of independence have vanished, leaving only in their trails, despair and stagnation. The blame here is heaped on poor leadership by the 'nationalists, the first generation of elected leaders and legislators of our semi-independent nation' who 'saw the nation as a prostrate victim to be ravished' (*You Must Set Forth at Dawn*, p. 48).

In his analysis, Hunjo censors post-independence African leaders for their inability to re-invent the colonial state in such a way that will make it inclusive, participatory and less alienating. The colonial structure was undoubtedly modelled on Western values and development was seen from the prism of how the state would advance European interests by incorporating the colonies into the orbit of global economy. That economy was defined, shaped and dominated by Europe and North America. Hunjo also blames the elite for their lack of will to replicate in Africa the indices of development they see in the metropolitan centres of Europe.

However, Hunjo's concept of development is rather Western-centric and material-oriented rather than being human-centred as advocated by Simala in the first chapter. Simala sees development not in a material and hegemonic sense, but in human, culturally specific terms. Like Adeoti, however, Hunjo also sees in Soyinka's representations, the fact that dictatorship has reached its wits end in African politics, being forced to retreat from one nation to the next in the last two decades of the Twentieth century. Hunjo examines *You must Set Forth at Dawn* 'to identify the political thinking template of postcolonial African leaders'. In Hunjo's view, Soyinka believes that the kind of education and political orientation that the post-independence African leaders have can only stifle development because they are intended to preserve rather than dismantle colonial legacy of exploitation of the majority by a few. Presenting textual evidence, Hunjo notes that there has been a disjuncture between the aspirations of the ordinary citizens and the preferences of the ruling elite since independence, a reality that has done so much to impede social growth and create tension.

In his exemplification of critical discourse analysis, Hunjo submits that Soyinka employs lexical items that clearly portray postcolonial leaders as 'political misfits' who ought not to have been trusted with the administration of states. These lexical items are identified in *You must Set Forth at Dawn* and used to demonstrate the prevalence of profligacy, tyranny, corruption, and other anti-development agencies. The leaders are depicted in the autobiographical narrative as a 'vicious breed' who nurse no love for the citizens. They are also 'self-centred, ostentatious, corrupt, and wasteful'. As they subordinate national interests to personal ones, they turn out to be 'parochial self-builders' and not 'nation builders'. They are not genuinely committed to the projects of decolonisation, democratisation and development, three cardinal engagements of post-independence African regimes. He concludes that there is no alternative route to development other than democratic rule and in this crucial realisation lies the future of Africa. Therefore, it is important that African leaders in the Twenty-first century should re-examine their vision of governance in the urgent task of achieving true liberation and development. One step in this regard is for leaders to free their countries from endless dependence on the international monetary agencies of the developed world such as the World Bank, International Monetary Fund, Paris Club and so on. To him, no African nation can attain the dream of independence if, through the actions or omissions of its leaders, such a country is still economically dependent on, politically subservient to, and culturally imitative of Europe and America.

The continuous engagement of African literature, especially poetry, with history and politics is also explored by Sule Egya. Poetry is not just a means of information, but also a means of observing and critiquing events in a society. Like other genres of literature, poetry records people's experience and critically engages their daily realities. Thus, the chapter focuses on African written poetry especially of the post-Senghor/Soyinka/Kunene generation. Included in the study are poets such as Niyi Osundare, Jack Mackpanje, Kofi Anyidoho, and members of the generation(s) after them.

In his survey of written African poetry from its nationalist origin to the Twenty-first century, Egya argues that the young generations of poets, like their predecessors during the early independence years are 'concerned about the seemingly bleak fate of the continent'. According to him, one of the recurring issues in African poetry across generations is how ordinary people can reap the benefits of independence through a better political and socio-economic deal than they have at the moment. He concentrates on the works of the 'emerging' or 'new' poets. This classification is quite slippery as it is sometimes difficult to strictly delineate the time, style and subject that separate these 'emerging' or 'new' poets from the established ones.

Politics is a recurring concern of the emerging poets just as it dominated the works of their predecessors. Thus, a sense of innovation and continuity defines the poetics of the new poets and poems among whom are Fungisayi Sasa: 'Anthem' (Zimbabwe), Dzekashu Macviba: 'Exodus' (Cameroon), Abigail George: 'Orange Farm on the 7'oclock News' (South Africa), Olu Oguibe: 'A Song from Exile' (Nigeria), and Nnimmo Bassey: 'Intercepted' (Nigeria). These poets and others are very strident in their criticism of the establishment as they oppose misrule in their countries. To escape from indices of leadership failure at home, some of the poets have relocated to the Western world, thus, cultivating the angst of exile. As Egya argues from a sociological perspective, exile is a condition imposed by failure of governance at home.

These new poets who emerged in the last decade of the Twentieth century discover early on the social responsibility of the poet and they see the art of poetry as a popular art, not for the court of the kings but more appropriately for the market places, using accessible diction and familiar tropes. This view of poetry accords with that of Niyi Osundare, one of the leading voices in contemporary poetry. The tone of their works is as agitating and protesting as that of the nationalists who expressed yearning for decolonisation. Thus, there is an observable link between the decolonisation project of the early African poets and the concerns with democratisation, good governance and development of the emerging poets.

With influence from Marxist theory of social change, the poets draw artistic elements from indigenous poetic traditions. A constant echo is disenchantment with the status quo. They challenge the reigning order in their countries because they see much of the problem as being largely political; once the governance question is addressed all other dreams will be realised.

However, while the old and the new generations are united by their social discontent, they differ in a significant respect. Poets of the second generation, it is observable, are optimistic about the possibility of social change in Africa, through a revolt of the masses after a programme of conscientisation. The new poets are, on the other hand, pessimistic because the continent seems to be sinking deeper and deeper into crisis, despite the deluge of protest poetry and *agit prop* drama. This pessimism creates a sense of alienation and, perhaps, informs their embrace of exile. They indict the elite of collusion with the state apparatus to oppress and inflict suffering on the masses. The image of a country going backwards in development terms is painted by Abigail George when she writes:

> Counting every two steps forward we take three back We move forward and backward like a river seemingly with ease ('Orange Farm on the 7 O'clock News', lines 22–3)

To the poets, if the present is precarious, the future is being further jeopardised; the phenomena of the child-soldier, out-of-school children, street urchins, unemployed youths, baby-making factories, teenage pregnancy, child trafficking indicating a wasted past, an endangered present and a bleak future. As Egya writes of Fungisayi Sasa's 'Anthem', which is significantly true of the poetry of the new generation, she paints a picture of a nation despoiled by its few political elites who though wicked, corrupt and mindless, pose as great leaders and thinkers, even as messiahs, notwithstanding the backward state of affairs.

Exile may offer the emigrant poets no respite from the troubles of the homeland as they suffer the estrangement of being abroad. The promised land of Europe and America disappointingly turns out to be another Egypt. As Egya acknowledges, the condition of exile is registered in their poetry in the tropes of 'dispersal', 'migration', 'otherness', 'multiculturalism' and 'eclecticism'.

In the final analysis, it is clear from Egya's survey of the works of the new generation of African poets that Africa's crisis of development is traceable to mis-governance and bad leadership. Therefore this problem has to be tackled before the continent can overcome the menancing incubus of stasis over the five previous decades. This is also the position of other contributors, including Ogundipe.

Ogundipe in 'African Literature and the Anxiety of Being in the Twenty-first Century' presses the leadership question further in his study of new writings from Africa and the challenges of existence. His focus is on how contemporary African literature has articulated the challenges of living in Africa in the Twenty-first century with specific attention paid to the new generation of writers who also feature in Egya's essay. Arising from the discourse are issues of identity, writers and social vision, literature and new media technology as well as the language of African literature. The diversity of language actually implicates *ab initio*, the heterogeneity of African literature while the new technology for the production of literary experienced across the globe has necessitated a re-definition of literature so as to accommodate the printed text, the new media, film, internet, and so on. As Ogundipe observes, the nature of African literature is as problematic as the identity of the continent. The identity question is directly or indirectly tied to the question of language; hence, contemporary African literature, which is mostly produced in European languages – English, French and Portuguese – has the problematic task of representing local experience in a 'foreign' language. Thus, African literature manifests hybridism in its 'glocalised' appeal.

The language issue has been variously addressed since the 1960s by Obi Wali (1963) who warns about the 'dead end' of African literature produced in European languages, Ngugi wa Thiong'o (1986) and Akinwumi Isola (2010) who advocate for African literatures in African languages. Alain Ricard (2004) also contributes to the debate. Other writers like Soyinka and Achebe did not mind using English so long as it could communicate their thoughts to their targeted audience across the world. The implication of this is that contemporary African literature, from the beginning, is characterised by a multiplicity of subjects, plurality of voices, and divergence of literary styles. As Ogundipe submits, a way of making sense and realising the essence of African literature is to recognise literature (oral, written, performed or screened) in indigenous African languages as a valid part of the people's literary experience. Such works, he argues, should have as much attention as, if not greater than, those produced in foreign languages.

Writers must contend with new challenges facing the continent if their products are to remain relevant and topical. These include child-soldiers, child trafficking, insurgency, proliferation of militias, rising unemployment, social inequality, environmental degradation, climate change, flooding, famine, ethnic chauvinism, religious intolerance and commercialisation of religion among other social irritants that hold disturbing implications for the future of the continent. New writers are already rising to the challenge, using different narrative modes, mostly eclectic and daringly experimental. In these new writings, sex and sexuality are freely and openly expressed as part of the new ethos of globalisation and cosmopolitanism. Here, the euphemism of traditional narrative is replaced with unabashed 'pornography'.

Against the backdrop of these challenges and their negotiations in the contemporary literary imagination, Ogundipe makes a case for an all-inclusive concept of African literature that promotes regional integration and pan-African ideals. Besides, he calls for a review of the status quo that privileges literary productions in European languages since such a situation creates a feeling of otherness and marginality. Ogundipe also advocates for greater interests in oral literature and indigenous performance traditions especially in the production, scholarship and criticism of African literature. This implies that the works of griots, minstrels, ballad singers, chanters and traditional poets who use indigenous languages to practice their arts should be included in the new literary experience. The frontiers of orality/performance should also be extended to accommodate other texts and media – television, film, internet and so on. Information and communication technology offers a new paradigm of knowledge dissemination and cultural documentation. The transition from traditional print culture to an electronic 'hyper text' or the digital form is imperative in this regard as writers, critics and scholars of African literature are expected to take advantage of the possibilities of transferring texts across multiple media. In this regard, the future of African literature, perhaps, is online as Ogundipe concludes:

> In the search for a viable path for the future of African literature, therefore, well-crafted vision of the future and effective strategies to engender transformation are imperative. This raises the practical application of the digital space, the internet and related innovative technology as new paradigms of knowledge for the African literary engagement.

Like Simala in Chapter one, Sola Ogunbayo in the final chapter,an analysis of prophetic myths in selected fiction of Ben Okri, emphasises the need to take a backward glance at the past and peep into the future through the framework of mythology. Myth is presented as a universal and timeless phenomenon that flourishes in the process of man's quest for meaning of events and explanation of things. According to the author, myth is essentially a product of imagination;

hence, it is the precursor of modern day literary productions and it has influenced countless written texts over centuries. Myths contain events that are probable in human behaviour even though it is essentially fictional. Ogunbayo submits that myth can be useful in predicting the future, judging from the possibilities encapsulated in its timeless and universal codes. 'The future in this regard, is a kind of behaviour and it can be foretold through the creation of myth', writes Ogunbayo. Myth can be used as a foreknowledge of probable occurrence in future. Like Simala he observes that myths deploy human and non-human characters to create events that are universal and timeless, hence, futuristic. Myth becomes a tool from the ancient past through which the future of Africa can be negotiated.

Ben Okri deploys myths as prophesy in two of his works. These are *Astonishing the Gods* and *In Arcadia*. In the analysis, Ogunbayo shows that Okri uses 'recurring pattern of human imagination and repetitive historical happenings to form archetypal templates that foreshadow the future'. In the two texts, the archetypes that stem from myth manifest through the form of 'quest' journey motif, adventure, pain and reward. The author argues that poor governance is a mythical construct that is associated with those who preside over the state. He also views kidnapping, terrorism, corruption and other ills in the same light. He suggests that the solution lies in a dialogue of myths.

Consequently, in his submission, a myth becomes an aperture into many layers of meanings through dynamic interactions of imaginations; a myth can be used to 'anticipate and predict the consequences of a current myth'.

One comforting fact worthy of note is that in his reconstruction of myth in *Astonishing the Gods* and *In Arcadia*, Ben Okri paints a pleasing picture of Africa. Africa is seen as a continent of hope with heartwarming potentials for progress and innovation. In the two works, myth is used to address local problems of governance as well as those associated with the pressures of incorporating the continent into Western cultural and economic hegemony, encapsulated as globalisation.

Arcadia, a trenchant metaphor for the future, represents individual and collective quest for a new Africa through the journey motif. Arcadia is a mythic form encapsulating the past, the present and the future of Africa. As Okri depicts it, Arcadia is the cherished desire of every human being in life and at the level of the community; it is a kind of 'serenity' affected by working democratic governance which offers, as its natural fruits, development. Arcadia is perfection, orderliness, harmony, and corporeal beauty. These are ideals which Okri believes that Africa should strive for in the years ahead.

In *Astonishing the Gods*, myth is registered as a trope of change, a principal and permanent law of nature. Okri shows that for there to be changes from present hardship, there is the need to puncture the myth of power and hegemony constructed by the present ruling elite whom he regards as 'the Gods'. To 'astonish (defeat and displace) the 'Gods', according to Ogunbayo, is to de-mythologise them and challenge their invincibility. From the analyses, it is evident that both texts are useful in enhancing our understanding of past events and current trends as they are symbolically woven together by Okri to anticipate the future of Africa; a future of pleasant possibilities. Ogunbayo also shares the view of Simala and Egya on the need for Africa to look inward and be self-reliant, rather than perpetually depend on foreign aids and loans.

In summary, one thing that is clear from all the six essays is that there are many dimensions of African experience in history, culture and politics captured by different generations of African writers. Not only do the writers dissect the continent's problems, using different idioms; some have taken steps to proffer saner paths to a better future for the people, hoping that the targeted agents of change would bring about the desired transformation. The task would involve the ruling elite and the ordinary people on the streets; the rich and the poor, men and women, youths and adults, urban dwellers and rural peasants.

Running through the essays is a demonstration of the intersection of literature and politics from the colonial era to the postcolonial present, invoking African literature as a platform for mediating the tensions of public sphere. However, while some African writers across generations and gender re-present the continent from a pessimistic perspective, some portray it in optimistic light. What is assured from their interventions is the continuous relevance of literature to the task of seeking genuine democracy, good governance and human centred-development. This mission certainly bridges the gulf between the past of Africa and its future. It also binds, inseparably, the continent's literary arts with its complex social contexts.

References

Isola, Akinwumi, 2010, 'Interview', in Gbemisola Adeoti, ed., *Voices Offstage:* Nigerian Dramatists on Drama and Politics, Ibadan: Kraft Books Limited

Osundare, Niyi, 2007, *The Writer as Righter: The African Literature Artist and His Social Obligations*, Ibadan: Hope Publications Limited.

Ricard, Alain, 2004, The Languages & Literatures of Africa: The Sands of Babel, Oxford: James Currey.

Soyinka, Wole, 2006, *You Must Set Forth At Dawn*, Ibadan: Bookcraft.

wa Thiong'o, Ngugi, 1986, *Decolonising the Mind: The Politics of Language in African Literatures*, London: James Currey.

Wali, Obiajunwa, 2008 [1963], 'The Dead End of African Literature?', in Tejumola Olaniyan, *Theory,* Oxford: Blackwell Publishing.

1

Orality, Modernity and African Development: Myth as Dialogue of Civilisations

Inyani Simala

Introduction

The desire to understand pressing issues such as modernity and development is not made any easier by competing and different knowledge domains. None of these domains offers a single and comprehensive answer to what is happening around us. Thus, my concern in this chapter is to discuss the various ways in which orality provides an indispensable, eternally-expanding guide to reading, writing, living and creating the African world of the past, present and future. It is my contention that what has generally been dismissed as myth is a complex intellectual reflection on civilisations in contact, conflict and conversations in response to modernity. Explaining the intimate correlation between orality, myth and modernity, the chapter demonstrates that myths belong to traditional oral philosophy, which can be harnessed as indigenous resources in dealing with development challenges facing the African continent.

Myth is central to oral tradition in Africa. Despite the important roles being played by myth and the ubiquity of this oral form, its importance on the continent is yet to be properly acknowledged. Interestingly, myth stands as a representation of the collective experience of the African people on the one hand and as a reconstruction of their consciousness induced by engagements with modernity on the other. Whereas African orality has been regarded as myth, and nothing more, by many scholars, its mix of multiple voices, fusion of personal and communal historical experiences, fragments of narrativity, its riveting imagery and layered allusiveness all remain hallmarks of a response to modernity.

While some scholars have been conscious of the place of myth in African orality, they have too often missed its cues on the challenges of modernity. Consequently, many scholars have treated African orality superficially and contemptuously as largely mythical and not modernist. Yet, African orality explores, recreates and seeks meanings in human experience, contemplating and celebrating its diversity, complexity and the strangeness of interactions of civilisations at different times. While much of what has been said so far, mostly non-African scholars, represents the notion of traditional myth, a closer re-examination of oral tradition reveals that it is not marginal to issues defining modern society, including science and technology. However, with the turn to orality, there is a growing consciousness of cultural identity and myth is becoming a domain of great intellectual interest to various scholars in African studies.

The purpose of the essay, therefore, is to increase the visibility, sustainability and acceptability of orality as a form of indigenous knowledge by connecting it with ideas about modernity. It argues that the challenge of understanding today's fast-changing world is how to balance and connect knowledge from different perspectives through partnership, collaboration, innovation, integration and communication based on active cultivation of dialogue between different communities.

While acknowledging the fact that there are alternative forms of knowledge and cultural transmission outside the sphere of literate modernity, the paper concludes that unlike in the West where written culture is a sign of modernity, the oral-tradition in Africa, as a people's wisdom and philosophy, becomes a marker for modernity, an ever-moving point marking off our own present from a long past. African orality also represents the depth and achievements of the people's culture. It forms an important contextual basis within which we come to terms with the challenges of development facing the continent in the twenty-first century and beyond.

Myth–Orality Nexus and the 'Other' Modernity

Despite the fact that in Africa, orality is as significant as modernity, the concept has remained largely neglected and that accounts for many of the myths characterising it. Whereas, orality engages the concepts of dialogue of civilisations and modernity, this reality has been lost through superficial and contemptuous analyses, misinterpretations and distortions. Yet, emphasising the roles of myth and orality as discourses in systematic exploration of African reality, and their responses to modernity, can help us understand them as a projection of a 'future history' of the world and the need for civilisations to dialogue.

The development of African society and its values is reflected in orality and myth. This is because there is a particular worldview associated with myth and orality on the continent. The two are important. They narrate histories of transition as they are themselves histories of language, culture, society and tradition. As a living embodiment of African metaphysical principles and self-consciousness, orality and myth are guides to reading, writing, living and creating the African world. Myth and orality are in a symbiotic relationship in Africa; with the former being ubiquitous in oral tradition, and the latter almost always based on the former. Both belong to traditional African philosophy.

As a growing consciousness of cultural identity, myth and orality offer multiple perspectives on the spatial and temporal nature of life and its civilisations. They are a repository of potentially radical and subversive sentiments on encounters of civilisations. The two are emerging as domains of great intellectual interest on the continent. The narratives stand both as a representation of the concrete facts of the people's collective experience and as a reconstruction of the consciousness induced by that experience of engagements with the idea of modernity, with multiple implications that challenge the existing influence of individual leaders, groups of people, institutions and whole communities.

As a historical bridge between the past and the present, orality offers multiple perspectives on the spatial and temporal nature of African life and its civilisations. Thus, African orality is an enlightened 'text' invested with social and political capital which throws light on the paradigm of civilisations in dialogue. The inclusion of African orality in the civilisations in dialogue debate is at once decentring and a critique of the hegemonic and oppressive Western systems of thinking and knowing that define the modernity paradigm and exclude Africa. Exploring epistemology in African orality privileges the oral philosophy that has existed on the margins of modern literate society and at the same time demonstrates how the two can blend in a creative way.

Myth and orality in Africa have important contributions to make to modern discourses and creative productions. They straddle tradition and change as they connect Africans to memory and ancestors. They are a historical bridge across the past and the present of Africa. While acknowledging and appreciating the massive canvass of philosophical and epistemological foundations of myth and orality in Africa, and their unique historical value, the two have come under the sustained imperialising and subordinating power of the written word. As a consequence of the discriminatory tendencies of literate modernity, the two are placed low on the hierarchy of intellectual, cultural and civilisational achievement.

However, modernity is not a purely Western phenomenon. Even though Western modernity is hegemonic and homogenising, there is a multiplicity of modernities parallel to Western modernity. Myth and orality in Africa articulate different forms of African identity and self-consciousness, their particular unity and distinction from the 'Other'. They have profound and far-reaching messages on the clash and dialogue of civilisations. Both are important in understanding and addressing modernity challenges facing the African continent, including universalising culture, global civilisation and the paradox of development.

Myth, Modernity and the Development Question in Africa

At present, perhaps, no challenge is more complex than the development question and its effects on Africa. As the global community of scholars explores the problem and its effects, their deliberations are situated at the confluence of science, technology, management and policy. However, the problem of development as seen in the need for improved quality of life occurs on multiple spatial and temporal scales. The effects of this reality respect no boundaries of whatever kind. Likewise, we need knowledge and institutions that defy any boundary limitations. This implies that if we are to respond effectively to the challenges of development in Africa, cross-disciplinary answers to the problem must be sought beyond any one dominant and hegemonic narrative.

At the dawn of independence in the 1960s, 'development' was regarded as the most central mission of the new African states. For the last five decades, many suggestions and proposals of how to tackle the development question in Africa have been produced. Development programmes were formulated based on the ideas that political leaders, planners and influential pressure groups held about a desirable nation, how it should be governed and the roles of the citizens in effecting socio-political changes. An ideology emerged that required the subordination of virtually all interests of national concern to the imperative of development. The aim of most African governments was to achieve improved standards of living through the eradication of ignorance, disease and poverty. The rhetoric of development itself, however, was deeply infused with the notion of nation-building, a term which had become pivotal in the entire vocabulary of postcolonial politics.

Though some of the strategies pursued by independent African governments initially delivered high levels of economic growth, none of them proved capable of achieving to sustained and sustainable development. The main aims of a majority of governments at independence were social justice, individual liberty and economic independence. The logic then was that these objectives were realisable in a strong and growing economy that could guarantee a stable society. Development planning placed almost exclusive emphasis on the role of physical capital in furthering economic progress. This marked the genesis of the materialist meaning of development that characterised much of Africa in the first decade of independence.

Pioneer pan-Africanists like Jomo Kenyatta, Léopold Sédar Senghor, Julius Nyerere, Kenneth Kaunda, Gamal Nasser, Nelson Mandela, Haile Selassie, Eduardo Mondlane and Sekou Touré were not only political leaders but also excelled as intellectuals who experimented with great original and imaginative ideas. Such ideas include Mwalimu Julius Nyerere's *Ujamaa* (Socialism), Kenyatta's *Harambee* (Pulling together), and Kwame Nkrumah's *Consciencism*. These great thinkers initiated nation-building development policies that were driven by tremendous seriousness of purpose and desire to see Africa become self-reliant and interdependent in its desire to gain dignity in the world. While not looking only to Western civilisation for paradigms of change and progress, they were ideologically innovative, philosophically independent and borrowed from both indigenous culture and foreign influence. Even though most of their experiments did not deliver sustainable development dividends, these were heroic attempts to find their own routes towards self-reliance and socialist egalitarianism rooted in indigenous African civilisation.

It can be argued that development planners have not been able to transform African societies from their unsatisfactory conditions due to their failure to have a clear image of the significant components or factors that make up African societal structure. No African community can develop without paying considerable attention to crucial cultural elements including myth and orality. Looked at separately, these components may not strike one as being central to any form of development. However, the relative strength of each can only be appreciated in the influence they have on each other and their overall impact on development. There can be no doubt that African development can change for the better if these factors are harnessed as resources that closely interact. That is what informed the original African Renaissance of the 1930s which would later on be elaborated upon by Thabo Mbeki and other African revivalists in the 1990s.

Whereas popular participation was desirable as early as the late 1960s, the dynamics of human factors as well as the importance of language, culture and participatory communication as building blocks of African societies were not duly acknowledged. Instead, over the years, development planners and managers of the process stressed the need for economic efficiency, national planning programmes, efficient organisation of production, and the necessity of techno-bureaucratic methods. But Africa is a continent of many civilisations,and therefore needs a diversification of its outlook on development.

During the 1970s, the development literature became dominated by the concept of satisfying the basic needs of poor households and providing them with opportunities for self-enhancement. Given that world-wide economic growth in the 1960s did not 'trickle-down' to the majority in the third world (mostly African countries) the need was perceived to attack the problem of poverty more directly. This emphasis led to greater global support for a rural focus in development strategy and planning. This approach did not deliver and as a consequence, development expectations aroused by the independence euphoria in Africa had evaporated by the close of the 1970s.

In the last two decades of the Twentieth century, the global development debate has largely been defined by neo-liberal theories and prescriptions for reform. In Africa, in response to the economic downturn and debt crisis of the 1970s, the International Monetary Fund and the World Bank pressed for structural-adjustment packages fashioned on the theory and practice of neo-liberalism. More than just being an economic theory, neo-liberalism is also a political theory.

Where neo-liberals have called for economic conservatism and the preeminence of the market, they have also supported the theory of a minimal state. Indeed, central to the critique of structural adjustment in the South is the commonly cited evidence that neo-liberal packages have in fact seriously exacerbated poverty levels and distributional inequalities.

However, the practical implications of this dialogue, particularly from a policy and research perspective, are considered somewhat tenuous. Whereas critics of the neo-liberal school have highlighted real weaknesses of the dominant economic paradigm, others suggest that the strength of the critics' perspective has been in their theoretical and social critique of neo-liberalism, rather than in their articulation of a cogent and defensible alternative. Indeed, the predominant focus of this critical literature on the social failings of neo-liberal reform has spurred charges that it has merely challenged imperfect mainstream models from the perspective of equally unsustainable interventionist or welfarist strategies that still leave too much in the hands of the state. Scepticism about the contribution of the critics of neo-liberalism has also been reinforced by recent historical trends: the dramatic failure of socialist economies has undermined proposed alternatives to a market-oriented approach.

The dismal economic record of structural-adjustment policies and the perception that they have had far-reaching negative social effects have fuelled broad-based criticism of these policies. In the developing world, concerns about the social implications of the neo-liberal agenda have been expressed through extensive research on the practical burden that economic reforms have placed on grass-roots groups. Among the reforms witnessed across Africa were deregulation of economies, trade liberalisation, export promotion, currency devaluation, strengthening of the financial sector, and public-sector reform. Through such reforms, neo-liberalism took root in many African countries and came to inform development strategies, including social-cultural policies. Consequently, social-cultural policies became marginalised and have, therefore, remained implicitly separate and subordinate to overarching economic priorities.

The dominant development model that has been gradually adapted in Africa is the Western one, which is founded on materialistic ideology, secularism, consumerism, individualism and modern science and technology. This kind of development is contrary to that advocated by UNESCO in 1982, which defined development as a complex, holistic and multidimensional process, which goes beyond mere economic growth and integrates all the dimensions of life and energies of a community, all of whose members must share in the economic and social transformation effort, and in the benefits that result.

While most of Africa is generally considered to be economically underdeveloped, it is culturally rich. It is this realisation that compels us to re-think the tendency of limiting development to the techno-economic field alone. The socio-economic development of Africa certainly does not and ought not to follow the development course of the West in all respects. Whereas, most of Africa might not have what the West has, such as usable natural resources, capital accumulation, technological superiority, an industrial base, Western rationality, and so forth, the continent has what the West may not have – cultural resources. Many African communities possess unique cultural values and indigenous languages that can be harnessed and utilised in the process of the mobilisation and organisation needed to pursue the goal of sustainable development. It is the nature of the relationship between culture and development that raises many of the important issues engaged in this chapter.

Over the years, development approaches and development policy have been ill-conceived for failing to pay adequate attention to cultural identity. As a consequence, the importation of an alien model of development has led to the impoverishment of the moral and spiritual basis of African societies. Efforts to offer an alternative development model that is rooted in indigenous culture, and which could be more suited in the local situation have not been successful. Many obstacles have been cited for this failure. First, culture is an abstract concept that is difficult to define with precision and general acceptance. Second, in many African countries, the formulation of a cultural policy has raised a set of complicated problems that include content, application, cost, implementation, benefit, sustainability and evaluation. The third issue revolves around the question: how much of their resources can African countries commit to cultural preservation, promotion and development?

The above scenario has not acknowledged and appreciated African culture as a precondition for development. Rather, culture has been viewed as being in opposition to development. However, the experience of the last five decades shows that for development to occur, a complex set of factors needs to fall into place, and economic growth is only one of these factors. Culture is a factor whose role has either been misunderstood or not understood at all. Higher levels of economic growth do not necessarily translate into increased social well-being or the eradication of poverty for millions of people excluded from development. Economic growth is no longer equated with development; rather, development has multiple dimensions.

The key challenge is not only to understand the complex and multi-directional links among the various dimensions of development but also to identify the ways in which these can be reinforced through appropriate public strategies and policies. Indeed, one of the key concerns of development theory and research has been to understand how public policies and programmes can be designed to address both persistent and newly emerging development problems.

With the broadening of the concept of development in the recent past, it is increasingly acknowledged that public policies in such areas as oral culture have, in their own right, a direct bearing on the nature, direction, and outcomes of a country's development efforts. It is this realisation that has led both governments and development agencies all over the world to recognise the need to put people at the centre of development and to give development a human face. They have begun to advocate strategies that explicitly address social-development needs. According to the new thinking, development processes are fundamentally a question of human development, which includes history, culture, communication and participation. Yet, there has been relatively little research that systematically examines the roles and impacts of cultural policies in African development.

Recognition of the changing nature and importance of cultural policy is reflected in the emergence at the international level of a distinct discourse on social development. Thus, the final report of the World Conference on Social Development (United Nations 1995) emphasised the need to promote dynamic, open, free markets, while recognising the need to intervene in markets to the extent necessary to prevent or counteract market failure, promote stability and long term investment, and harmonise economic and social development. There is a growing consensus around the concept of people-centered development, which places culture at the centre of development thinking, with emphasis on popular participation. It is argued that all important factors of development be put on an equal footing with the macroeconomic angles which to date have been given priority.

Opposition to the priority given to economic concerns has led to a renewed emphasis on social-cultural development. Beginning in the early 1990s, and in large part driven by the backlash against narrowly defined economic reforms and perspectives, strong support has emerged for a more balanced approach to development, one that integrates both a social-cultural and an economic objective without subordinating one to the other.

Africa, Myth and the Dialogue of Civilisations Narrative

Mythology has had great influence on African life and ways of thinking. Dealing with the lore of Africans, myths have intriguing tales and themes including dialogue of civilisations. As oral art forms, and with captivating characters and episodes, myths from all periods and from all parts of Africa are fascinating. There are similarities between themes, characters, incidents, and even details, in the mythologies of countries that are widely separated by distance. What this means is that different peoples throughout the continent were faced with similar situations, similar phenomena of nature, asked themselves similar questions, and answered them in much similar ways making clear their ideals, their mode of life, their state of civilisation.

Just as there was great flowering of myths and legends in various parts of Europe and Asia, Africa too had its own story about its ancient civilisations. The complexity and paradox of mythology in Africa is comparable to the accounts of the myths and legends of India as told in the great Mahabharat and the Ramayana

Like the mythology of China which accepted influences from neighbouring areas in order to fulfil the needs of the people, myths in Africa were not insular to such effects. And just like the Greeks who descended from the Indo-European tribes, there are African communities who trace their origin to disparate communities who settled in different valleys, hills and along the coasts.

It is often pointed out that certain river valleys have been cradles of civilisation, and the valley of the Nile illustrates clearly what this signifies. Egypt produced one of the earliest civilisations which flourished over the course of more than 3,000 years, going as far back as 4,000 BC. Mesopotamia, the prodigiously fertile plain from which the Tigris and Euphrates rivers flow, was the heartland of several ancient civilisations – Babylonian, Assyrian and Chaldean. It was the scene of mighty struggles of mountaineers against nomads, and of king against king. Perhaps, that is why the dominant tone of the Babylonian mythology is one of disillusionment. It is full of intentional ambiguities on man's position in the universe and his ultimate fate. The transitory nature of life is always felt in mythology (Robinson and Wilson 1976).

There is a renewed attention across disciplines to myth as a source of knowledge as interest grows and turns towards interpretation of human life. Scholars under the influence of interpretative traditions such as phenomenology, hermeneutics, cultural criticism, feminism and symbolic interactionism have developed a sort of literary consciousness, as they employ techniques that were once mostly associated with literary analysis and criticism. Newly preoccupied with forms of expression, literary devices, rhetorical conventions, and the reading and writing of texts of experience (including bodies, lives and literature), scholars now see the story in the study, the tale in the theory, the parable in the principle, and the drama in the life. The study of narratives has linked sciences with history, literature and everyday life to reflect the increasing reflexivity that characterises contemporary inquiry and furthers the postmodern deconstruction of the already tenuous boundaries among disciplines and domains of meaning.

A prevailing conceptualisation of narrative is that it is one of the many modes of transforming knowing into telling. It is the paradigmatic mode in which experience is shared and articulated. Narratives assume many forms; they are heard, seen and read; they are told, performed, painted, sculpted and written. Human beings are immersed in narrative, telling themselves stories and recognising in their own stories, the stories of others. This re-conceptualisation of human beings as narrators and of their products as texts to be interpreted have been conditioned by empirical rather than narrative or biographical standards of truth and by a preoccupation with obtaining information at the expense of understanding expression.

Every age must re-criticize and reinterpret the great works of the past with view to finding new strands of relevance to particular cultural or intellectual contexts in order to keep them alive to humanity. Myths serve to account for life, unlike in the present when meta-narratives are constructed to explain events. Myths represent the collective imagination of a people or nation, not the inventions of any one person. It is worthy of note that myth is more than a historical and literary narrative. A re-reading of myth in Africa reveals that there is an alternative voice on the discourse of dialogue of civilisations. It is a connected pattern of ideas and evaluations which together constitute a key component of our modern world view. Despite this other meaning, the metaphoricity of myth has contributed to subdue its real meaning that has existed for many years before the current discourse on the clash of civilisations.

Samuel Huntington's idea of 'clash of civilisations' relies on a popularised version of the classical anthropological notion of culture as a complex, integrated whole' (Wimmer 2002: 19). Huntington's clash of civilisations is part of the meta-narrative of inter-relations that holds that culture explains the economic success and failure of whole nations. Implicit in this grand narrative is the traditional idea of cultural homogeneity and superiority which were limited to the colonial encounter, and 'helped legitimise colonial subjugation and exploitation'.

Huntington's 'clash of civilisations' (1993) has been treated as a great truth paradigm. The wealth and variety of discussions about the clash and the need for civilisations to dialogue demonstrate that there are many other voices discussing how power, abuse, dominance and inequality are enacted, reproduced and resisted in the modern world. However, the inadequacy ascribed to minority texts, voices and authors reveals the limiting ideological horizons of the dominant, ethnocentric perspective.

Lyotard (1984) alludes to the fact that such social knowledge may become instruments of social control as they abandon absolute standards, universal categories, and pragmatic social inquiry, being unaware of social differences, ambiguity and conflict. In his thesis on the decline of the meta-narrative, Lyotard voices a major theme of the postmodern turn: the decentring of the subject and the social world. Meta-narratives presuppose an ahistorical standpoint from which to understand the human mind, knowledge, society and history. The shift from meta-narratives to local narratives and from general theories to pragmatic strategies suggests that in place of assuming a universal mind or a rational knowing subject, we imagine multiple minds, subjects, and knowledges reflecting different social locations and histories.

Wimmer (2002:24) identifies four principal theoretical and methodological problems confronting the classical notion of culture. First, it does not give an answer to the problem of intra-cultural variation. Second, it cannot help to understand the relation between power and meaning. Third, its concept of human action is largely inadequate; Lastly, it does not offer an adequate tool to analyse processes of cultural and social change.

The idea that cultures are clearly discernible, bounded and integrated wholes becomes exclusionist and potentially dangerous for all those considered to belong to another culture (Wimmer 2002). Notions of multiplicity, hybridity, creolisation and multivocality have replaced the idea of cultural homogeneity and integration. Wimmer explains culture as an open and unstable process of the negotiation of meaning (2002:26). In the emerging thinking, discourse has replaced culture as the master term with such post-structuralists as Foucault trying to understand how, in a certain setting, multiple discourses criss-cross each other, overlap, develop into bundles of meaning, dissolve again and disappear. As the social world is synonymous with the coming and going of discourse (Foucault 1972:211), notions of economic relations, social structure and hierarchies of power are reduced to discourses on economic, social and political relations.

Myth in Africa epitomises this exclusion of minority discourse from the dominant dialogue of civilisation paradigms. Nevertheless, myth gives an account as seen from the margins of the clash of civilisations and the need for various civilisations to engage in dialogue. Situated in relation to contemporary discourses of 'the clash of civilisations' and the need for 'dialogue of civilisations', myth and orality in Africa provide a space in which questions about the nature of identity are most provocatively articulated. A critical-discursive articulation of alternative meanings in the texts can be re-read transformatively as indications and figurations of values radically opposed by the dominant culture.

Before foreign civilisations came to Africa, there were indigenous civilisations on the continent. Africans have existed on the continent since antiquity with a lot of economic, political, marital and other forms of interactions between different communities. Despite vague lines separating them, African peoples historically formed a socio-economic and cultural unit, welded together by a cultural identity with one another, a consciousness of a common history and common interests. These ways of living can only be understood and appreciated by identifying different communities and varying periods of their existence and interactions.

For instance, according to the *Periplus of the Erithrean Sea*, written around AD 110, the east coast of Africa was inhabited from a very early period by black people. From around AD 150, the various Bantu groups and families began to invade the east African coast, from both the south and the west. They established themselves along the rivers and in other cultivable places (Ylvisaker 1979). The centuries from 1000 BC to AD 400 constitute a Classical Age in which were laid the cultural and economic foundations on which the societies of Greater Eastern Africa were to build their institutions and livelihood for the following 1,500 years. It was an era of great transformation, which brought into being new forms of belief, culture and technology. The African Classical Age was marked by the full establishment of iron technology, the emergence of important new agricultural processes and technologies, and the spread of new religious and social ideals. In Greater Eastern Africa, the new cultural and economic dispensation was spread out toward the Indian Ocean seaboard from the interior. There were innovations and inventions which are inherently indicative of modernity.

The developments of the Classical Age of Greater Eastern Africa reveal the peoples of those regions as vibrant participants in the trends of world history. They engaged in the creation of more complex and more adaptive forms of agriculture. The Classical Age was a time of immense reshaping of belief, custom and livelihood. A myriad of complex histories of inter-ethnic interaction and economic and social change lie behind the social formations and economies that had come into being by the fourth century. The age lies at a key juncture of the defining and integrating themes of continental history. It was one of several regional stages of world history with three great, long-term historical themes integrating Greater Eastern Africa into world history: increasing establishment of more fully agricultural ways of life in regions that before then had successfully maintained either low-complexity food-producing livelihoods or less labour-demanding gathering-and-hunting economies; the spread of iron technology; and, commercial revolution (Ehret 1998:1).

European expeditions in Africa marked the beginning of imperialism and colonialism when once independent and vibrant kingdoms began to decline. With their modern weapons, and guided by greed and plundering intentions, the Europeans succeeded in ruining the formerly thriving African civilisations socially, politically and economically. The predominance of Western civilisation still witnessed today is not due to its superiority, but rather to all kinds of factors involved, some linked to ability, others to circumstance or chance.

There are political, moral and intellectual implications of all forms of encounters with otherness (Williams 1994). Western modernity has constantly meant the abandoning of part of one self. Though it has sometimes been embraced with enthusiasm, it has never been adopted without certain bitterness, without a feeling of humiliation and a profound identity crisis (Maalouf 2002:58–60). When European civilisation took the lead, African civilisations began to decline.

Through myth, Africans were not just reflecting on modernity but were actively involved in making it through actions and words. Various myths that are found across the continent should not mystify, but rather clarify people's experience of civilisations in contact and conflict. The discourse on the clash of civilisations shows that Africa has largely been excluded or ignored. Indeed, the regions on which Huntington focused did not include Africa. Indigenous communities in Africa had different, unique and perhaps unexpected experiences from what Huntington termed the 'clash of civilisations'. Indigenous communities on the continent embraced dialogue of civilisations long before the concept had been propounded by Huntington and his disciples.

Re-Reading Myth as Text

In order to demonstrate its considerable relevance and establish myth as a bridge linking antiquity and modernity, a fresh reading and re-writing of orality becomes imperative. Read as a ritual of ideological recognition, orality is the thread that ties myth, modernity and civilisation in African philosophy. Both myth and orality can be considered as 'collective memory' of the African people. The importance of memory is borne out by what Bartlett (1995) calls an effort after meaning, grounded in traces from the past, but an effort that actively shapes them in the present. Myth and orality can be described as a process of unfolding and revelation, with much that still remains hidden that can only be unravelled and understood with continued reading guided by clarification and explanation.

While a number of quite different strategies could be adopted to convey reading and understanding of a text, an attempt is made here to re-read and interpret myth and orality as transient and historical discourses that are part of African history and philosophy. Although analysing myth as oral history as an official document and repository of community knowledge poses many challenges, it becomes worthwhile because it yields precious experiences and insights into how Africans interpreted and understood the world around them. By engaging a variety of discourses, we have attempted to re-read the texts with a view to unveiling, legitimising and validating meaning that defies structures of power and domination that have hitherto characterised the scholarship.

Myth and orality are not each set up externally to each other, but are in an intricate and connected relationship, and this internal relationship is what constitutes the definition of the two as ideological forms of African philosophy. Thus, the analysis is not simply a historical approach to the texts, but a revolutionary understanding of the two forms of knowledge. This approach integrates ancient, contemporary and future history, challenging ideological assumptions by arguing that myth and orality in Africa do not just passively reflect experience.

Myth is a meta-metaphor with various levels and units having basic and contextual meanings which are extended and gradually developed. It is used to think and talk about experience. Metaphor is an important aspect of discourse in allowing users to reframe their perceptions, or see the world anew by offering new ways of looking at existing situations, while simultaneously acting as a bridge between a familiar and a new state. Metaphors can help to concretise vague and abstract ideas. They can also convey a large amount of information and foster new ways of looking at things. Metaphors can be used to persuade, reason, evaluate, explain, theorise, and offer new conceptualisations of reality (Semino 2008:22–32). This linguistic phenomenon of thinking about something in terms of something else not only contributes to rhetorical goals, but it is meant to produce responses that mirror a more general human response to existential condition of humankind (Lakoff and Johnson 1980).

Gordon (2008) identifies Africana philosophy as a species of Africana thought which involves theoretical questions raised by critical engagements with ideas in African cultures. In his view, before the invention of 'Africa', there existed in that modern space ancient civilisations which would be alien to the modern conceptualisation of the continent. Ancient and traditional African intellectual activities existed long before Greek philosophy. Africans were critical thinkers in their use of indigenous knowledge. Myth in Africa should be acknowledged as a reflection about the interactions, reactions and actions of different communities on the continent. By interacting with other civilisations, Africans must have encountered what Gordon (2008:14) calls 'modern concerns such as race, racism, and colonialism seriously, exploring problems of identity and social transformation, of the self and the social world, of consciousness and inter-subjectivity, of the body and communicability, of ethics and politics, of freedom and bondage'.

Myth is important as it is filled with philosophic meaning and explanation of human life and of the human soul. Unfortunately, the true nature of myth has become obscured by the diverse interpretations it has been given over the centuries, with much of what was originally advanced as scientific and psychological thinking degenerating into suspect magical practices. Myth carries a subconscious message that has aroused interest and respect in many great minds over the centuries. In order to understand myth, it is necessary to look at the historical and cultural background.

Myth in Africa is a work of painstaking intellectualism and ingenuity that reflects deeper workings of the African mind, insight and prophetic perception for dialogue of civilisations. It may sound ironical, ambiguous and paradoxical for myth to speak to a contemporary issue such as the clash of civilisations and the need for dialogue of civilisations. However, to grasp that other deeper meaning, attention has to be paid to details of articulation in an effort to arrive at its fullest possible understanding. This approach reveals that although concerns with clash of civilisations and the need for dialogue are more pronounced in contemporary society and culture, they are not a preserve of this era.

The primary ideological message of myth lies not in its explicit content, but in the attitude towards the reception it demands. It is this 'attitude towards information' which forms the basis for a response to other information, not necessarily literary, in the text. Thus inter-texts and pre-texts (Hutcheon 1999) are important in reading and looking for the metaphorical meaning that is not immediately apparent in myth by filling in gaps left without comprehensive facts so as to make the misty meaning visible.

Conclusion

From the foregoing, this chapter has attempted to critically examine the tangled and often contradictory relationship between myth, modernity and orality, and how the three impact on development in Africa. It has been argued that myth and orality in Africa are cultural spaces full of recollections and memories that the community occupies. They are an embodiment of the community's lived experiences and their ideological worldview. They express many types of relations that the African community had and serve as testimony through which the community reaffirms the values and traditions of the natural space that it occupies. These indigenous knowledge systems have been at the centre of the lives and livelihoods of Africans.

It has been established that myth and orality are laden with meanings and historical references. They interrogate and comment on the important theme of African responses to modernity, viewed in broad philosophical and social terms. However, despite being host to important human civilisations, Africa has been neglected in standard studies of world civilisations for decades. Instead, the trend in most historiography is only to signify Africa in terms of a mythical past. But through an analysis of the continent's orality, it can be demonstrated that Africans did not exist on the margins of history of civilisations.

The chapter has shown that there is not one accepted form of modernity. Rather, there are alternatives to the narrative and its chronology. Myth and orality bear layers of modern ideas and intellectual discourses among the African people. Their interactions and influences are part of the global narrative necessary to explicate the discourse on modernity.

Conventional and extremely dogmatic narratives of modernity that differentiate the universe between the 'West' and the 'rest', or 'modernity' and 'tradition/myth', or 'us' versus 'them', set the stage for clashes of civilisations, which are proliferating in the contest between champions of 'authenticity' and defenders of 'universalism' (Mirsepassi 2000:11), with the former as resistors of domination and the latter as promoters of prosperity. If modernity is to be taken as the search for meaning, then the world as a text has not one mode of reading, understanding and explaining.

At a time of unprecedented turmoil in world history, the myth of 'us' versus 'them' must be debunked. The current tensions understood as an imminent clash of civilisations are rooted in the historical trajectory of how modernity came into being, its causes and courses, its purpose, its ways and its ends. The clash of civilisations is as much a result of the failures of modernity as its consequence. There is the need for an authenticity discourse that represents a cultural attempt to reconfigure modernity and make it more inclusive and diverse, and less homogenising and totalising (Mirsepassi 2000:97). This discourse needs to be built around the critique of the Western conception of modernity and its discontents. The dominant narrative of modernity needs to be re-theorised in the light of increased awareness of the 'other' (Said 1994). There should be no undesirable 'other'.

In the contemporary world, other civilisations are very apparent and significant. The plurality of their voices and visions is what is required of the dialogue of civilisations. Instead of a universalist, intellectually naïve and simplistic worldview, hybrid versions of modernity should inform the dialogue. By opening up to new possibilities, modernity will welcome diversity, tolerance, inclusivity and openness to a dialogue of ideas. Modernity must open its spirit to a limitless diversity of voices, and make this the focus of its self-understanding (Mirsepassi 2000:35). It is this willingness to listen that will lead to dialogue, otherwise clashes with other civilisations will continue. Just like the Hegelian idealistic paradigm, the Western narrative of modernity is not a harmless intellectual idea; and it is this kind of discourse that threatens the 'other' into reactions and actions that are so often seen as anti-Western. Modernisation should not equal universalisation and homogenisation. There is not one kind of modernity in the world and no single narrow path leads to it.

Modernity should not be limited to the West and the contemporary alone. It is to be found in all places and at different times. It is a spatial and temporal socio-historical and literary narrative. It helps us engage in a dialogue with history. It can be treated as the site of the struggle of something new in the past and the present. The assertion that the West is shifting to a postmodern terrain need not presuppose the end of modernity. Modernity is not abruptly coming to an end. In most parts of the globe, modernisation remains the chief social goal. Modernity has not exhausted itself; it may be in crisis but it continues to shape the contours of our lives (Seidman 1994:1–2).

While acceptance of the challenge to development in Africa is increasing, there remains a lack of clarity over how exactly the problem should be addressed. What is not in doubt is the fact that understanding and tackling the development question requires insights from various natural, social and scientific disciplines drawing on diverse data sources. It is because of this fact that this study argues for a more inclusive approach that acknowledges the value of diverse perspectives in effectively responding to the challenge. It shows that myth in Africa contains a complex idea of dialogue of civilisations. While modern readers have been conscious of myth in Africa, they have too often missed its cues on the dialogue of civilisations. Yet, myth as orality explores, recreates and seeks meanings in human experience, contemplating and celebrating its diversity, complexity and strangeness of interaction.

Recent years have witnessed a remarkable renaissance in the study of orality in Africa in general and African myth in particular. While this rejuvenation of interest is welcome, it is our contention that there is a need to engage these forms of knowledge, which have, until now, been marginalised in modernist studies. Myth and orality should not be treated simply as provincial footnotes to African literature.

References

Bartlett, F.C., 1995, *Remembering: A Study in Experimental and Social Psychology*, Cambridge: Cambridge University Press.

Ehret, Christopher, 1998, 'An African Classical Age: Eastern and Southern Africa', in *World History, 1000 BC to AD 400*, Oxford: University Press of Virginia.

Finch, Charles, 1991, *Echoes of the Old Darkland, Themes from the African Eden*, Decatur, GA: Khenti.

Finnegan, Ruth, 1970, *Oral Literature in Africa*, Oxford: Clarendon Press.

Finnegan, Ruth 1977, *Oral Poetry*, Cambridge: Cambridge University Press.

Foucault, Michel, 1972, *The Order of Things*, New York: Pantheon.

Gordon, Lewis R, 2008, *An Introduction to Africana Philosophy*, Cambridge: Cambridge University Press.

Huntington, Samuel, 1993, 'The Clash of Civilisations', *Foreign Affairs*, 72 (3): 22-49.

Hutcheon, Linda, 1999, *A Poetics of Postmodernism: History, Theory, Fiction*, London: Routledge.

Lakoff, G. and Johnson, M., 1980, *Metaphors we Live By*, Chicago: Chicago University Press.

Lyotard, Jean-Francois, 1984, *The Postmodern Condition*, Minneapolis: University of Minnesota Press.

Maalouf, Amin, 2002, *On Identity*, London: Harvill Press. Translated by Barbara Bray.

Mirsepassi, Ali, 2000, *Intellectual Discourse and the Politics of Modernisation*, Cambridge: Cambridge University Press.

Robinson, H. S. and Knox Wilson, 1976, *Myths and Legends of All Nations*, New Jersey: Adams and Co.

aid, Edward, 1994. Orientalism?

Seidman, Steven, ed., 1994, *The Postmodern Turn: New Perspectives on Social Theory*, Cambridge: Cambridge University Press.

emino, Elena, 2008, *Metaphor in Discourses*, Cambridge. Cambridge University Press.

Williams, Eric, 1994, *Capitalism and Slavery*, Chapel Hill, NC: University of North Carolina Press.

Wimmer, Andreams, *Nationalist Exclusion and Ethnic Conflict*, Cambridge: Cambridge University Press.

lvisaker, Marguerite, 1979, *Lamu in the Nineteenth Century: Land, Trade, and Politics*, Boston University: African Studies Centre.

2

Requiem for Absolutism: Soyinka and the Re-visioning of Governance in Twenty-first Century Africa

Gbemisola Adeoti

Introduction

This chapter examines Wole Soyinka's notion and vision of governance in contemporary Africa as articulated through his dramaturgy. Over the years, Soyinka has remained an outstanding public intellectual and a committed writer whose philosophical reflections on the African world in the postcolonial era resonate across disciplines. In his creative *oeuvre* (plays, novels, poems, essays, films and music), Soyinka addresses the imperative of African development attained through democratic, people-driven modes of governance. He contends that the ascendancy of the culture of impunity in governance, even after independence from colonial rule, constitutes an obstacle to the continent's path to development. The reality of one party absolute rule or military government has subverted great expectations about the ideals of liberation nurtured by African nationalists during the anti-colonial struggles.

Drawing on textual illustrations from *The Beatification of Area Boy* and *King Baabu,* my essay submits that Soyinka advocates for a relentless war of attrition, fought on all fronts, including through cultural productions and drama, against despots, tyrants, autocrats and other purveyors of undemocratic rule, wherever they are found on the continent. In this regard, satire, the dominant theatrical and literary form of Soyinka's dramaturgy is employed in an onslaught against absolutism as the first step towards the recovery of popular will. This is demonstrated through the analyses of two plays produced on the threshold of the twenty-first century. Attention is also paid to the trope of cleansing or re-birth in the plays as it bears the prospects for re-inventing the African continent even in the face of systemic drawbacks.

In conclusion, the essay contends that the evolution of a just and humane social order in the twenty-first century is predicated on a sufficient knowledge of the inadequacies of the immediate past and present, against which a new order is to be erected. Soyinka's plays, and their sensitivity to politics, become a means of stock-taking toward developing a new democratic society.

Soyinka and the Absolute State

Soyinka is a close observer of, and a deeply involved participant in, the post-independence political history of Africa. His writing consistently engages the impurities of politics and governance on the continent, which have in turn stymied national development in many countries. From the traditional monarchical system, which condoned repressions of the slave trade era, to colonial administration that robbed the generality of the 'natives' of sovereignty and invested it in the hands of a few whose loyalty and obligations were towards Europe, Africa seems to be perennially haunted by authoritarian rule. Over five decades after independence, the battle against absolute rule has not been won decisively.

As evident from Soyinka's writings (novel, drama, poetry, essays, autobiographies and memoirs), the anti-colonial struggles of the Twentieth century and the concomitant 'independence' of many African countries presented opportunities for re-assessment towards seeking a new direction towards genuine nationhood and total liberation from imperialism. Unfortunately, the elites that succeeded the departing colonialists did not apprehend the above imperative as such. Hence, in place of a people-centred and people-driven mode of governance that would have launched the continent steadily on the path of socio-economic development, the elites frittered away the opportunities. They rather perpetuated the authoritarian governmental structures of colonialists that were *ab inito* arranged against the people they governed.

Nonetheless, the contradictions did not take long to unravel as fragile, delusive self-government began to collapse, giving way to one-party absolute rule or brazen military dictatorship in Nigeria, Ghana, Guinea, Equatorial Guinea, Sierra Leone, Togo, Côte d'Ivoire, Benin, Central African Republic, Burkina Faso, Gambia, Niger, Somalia, Zaire/DRC and Liberia among others. Within the first two decades of independence, militarism became a pandemic engulfing the continent like a wild fire in the savannah at the prime of dry season. Whereas, a democratic mode of governance would have, perhaps, unleashed energy for development and mediated the volatility of ethno-religious and social differences, the ascendance of the culture of impunity in governance constituted a great impediment to freedom and development as envisioned by nationalists in the days of anti-colonial struggles. In this dispensation, political spaces shrunk and human rights withered, leaving th silent and the excluded (sometimes, constitution a majority of the population), with violence as the only audible mode of communication with the state or in inter-group relations. As violence begat wilder and more virulent violence, Africa remained a cauldron of unending crises, buoyed by tyranny, external political manipulation, poverty, ethnic chauvinism, religious intolerance, poor infrastructure and illiteracy.

All this combined to register the failure of independence and have reverberated through the Twentieth century into the new millennium. Interestingly, Soyinka has consistently engaged these issues in his creative, critical and autobiographical writings (e.g. *Ibadan: the Penkelemes Years and You Must Set Forth at Dawn*). To him, the reality of personalized absolute rule manifested in one party government, a one-party dominated multi-party system, monarchism or outright military dictatorship, accounts largely for the inability of many African nations to realize their potentials, decades after flag independence.

For instance, in *A Dance of the Forests*, written in 1960 to celebrate the independence of Nigeria, his country of birth, Soyinka cautions that the future of the nation, and by extension Africa, is bleak with the kind of past and present defined by greedy elites, who bestride the dais of power in their countries like the proverbial colossus. In a sober but clairvoyant tone, the playwright depicts the fate of a people doomed to repeat the calamitous errors of history – a history marked by unending incarnations of autocrats, despots, dictators, tyrants and similar species. These characters find a concrete summation in Kongi, the eponymous hero of Kongi's Harvest. The crisis of governance that African nations experience shortly after independence is represented through the displacement of the traditional monarchical system of Oba Danlola by military dictatorship led by Kongi. Kongi's vacuous philosophy of 'ISMAism' is a cant for revolution and change. Pan-Africanists such as Marcus Garvey, W.E.B. Dubois, Kwame Nkrumah, Sekou Touré, Amilca Cabral, Aimé Cesaire and Herbert Macaulay among others considered revolutionary change as a way out of the bind of imperialism; Kongi's revolution is, however, a self-serving subversion of the ideal. No wonder it ends up in disaster, not only for him, but also for the people he leads. And that finds concrete illustration beyond the stage in the fate of tyrants like Idi Amin of Uganda, Siad Barre of Somalia, Mobutu Sese Seko of Zaire, and Ibrahim Babangida and Sani Abacha of Nigeria.

The danger posed by authoritarian rule to development is also the pre-occupation of Soyinka in *Madmen and Specialists*, a play inspired by the experience of his detention during the Nigerian civil war between 1968 and 1969; *Opera Wonyosi, Requiem for a Futurologist and A Play of Giants*. These plays have as their butts, recognizable historical figures like Idi Amin, Emperor Jean-Bedel Bokassa, and Shehu Shagari among others. *A Play of Giants*, for instance marks the fall of Idi Amin from power in Uganda in 1979 and hints at the beginning of the end for other autocratic regimes in Africa that were propped up by both sides of the ideological divide (America and Russia) during the Cold War era.

In these and other plays such as *Jero's Metamorphosis, The Bacchae of Euripides, The Scourge of Hyacinth, From Zia with Love, The Beatification of Area Boy and King Baabu*, Soyinka demonstrates absolute contempt for absolute rule, whether constituted by soldiers or civilians. He consistently ridicules despots and reduces to sand, their bloated castles of absolute power. He also advocates for an accountable and responsive government that derives its sovereignty and strength from the people. Hence, he exposes what he perceives to be wrong with Africa, using the instrumentality of satire, a literary device that seeks to cure aberrations through wit, irony, burlesque, parody, hyperbole and humour. He is often disturbed by the curious political dynamics of Africa characterized by oppression, corruption and wanton waste of public resources, in spite of all the positive interventions in the public spheres over the years. That reality has left many African states tethering precariously on the precipice of becoming 'failed states'. Kieh and Agbese (2008:13) capture the untoward state of affairs when they write:

> Africans who have been at the receiving end of state brutality, repression, corruption, abuse of power, dictatorship, and gross inefficiency would not hesitate to point out that the post-colonial state has been a total and abject failure. Decaying institutions, collapsed infrastructure and the virtual absence of the bureaucratic paraphernalia of the state in most rural areas have come to characterize the political landscape in much of Africa.

In summary, as scholarly studies have shown, the foregoing is responsible for political instability, economic stagnation and social upheaval in many African countries after independence, including Nigeria (Diamond et al. 1988; Oloruntimehin 2007). Soyinka's plays respond to this reality with laughter and indignation, hence, the constant adoption of satire. The aim is to expose and ridicule forces impeding Africa's true liberation and development.

The post-independent continent that engages Soyinka's dramaturgy is economically dependent on Europe, America and Asia. In terms of politics, even when there is a pretension or claim towards democracy, the state is authoritarian in nature and character. This is a perpetuation of the colonial state structure which Basil Davidson has described as 'rigid dictatorship in which government's policies and actions lack popular input' (1992:208).

As noted elsewhere (Adeoti 2006), whether in the Amorako republic of *From Zia with Love* or the Lagos city in *The Beatification of Area Boy*, where hoodlums exercise power or even in the Guatuna Empire of King Baabu, Soyinka depicts despots who masquerade as democrats. The targets are recognizable figures in Nigeria's political history at the twilight of the Twentieth century, but they are replicated in some other African countries. Nonetheless, in spite of the systemic setback, there are pointers within the template of dramatic conflicts to the inevitable limits of tyranny as indicated in the triumph of the underdog in *Th*

Beatification of Area Boy and the inglorious end of Basha Bash in *King Baabu*. Our task in the remaining part of this chapter is, therefore, to illuminate the playwright's notion of governance in contemporary Africa, and provide a basis for his postulations on the re-invention of the continent. The task is pursued through textual analyses of two plays: *The Beatification of Area Boy* and *King Baabu*.

The Beatification of Area Boy

In *The Beatification of Area Boy*, Soyinka adopts the operatic tradition already explored in *Opera Wonyosi and From Zia with Love*. The centring of violence as a means to survive and dominate is demonstrated in the conflict between agents of the state and hoodlums called 'Area Boys'. The state is portrayed by and large as a dome of villains. The soldiers who control the apparatus of power under the military regime and the hoodlums who rule the streets are similar in many respects. First, the soldiers constitute a minority of the population, but their command of the instruments of coercion is exploited to access power and impose their will on the majority. In the same vein, through violence, the Area Boys enforce their wills on their victims, the people. Second, the Area Boys survive on group solidarity which is similar to the espirit de corps of the military. Third, the military set out primarily to offer defence to the citizens, just as Area Boys offer protection to their clients. But in both cases, the protectors often turn out to be assailants. Fourth, uniformed men use state power to extort, dispossess and terrorize the people. The same constitute the *modus operandi* of Area Boys. To the satirist, the soldiers imperil order and stability as much as the Area Boys who are easily dismissed as 'bullies enforcers, thugs, extortionist, daylight robbers and drug addicts'. The soldiers and their civilian collaborators like Chief Kingboli and Professor Sematu use power to loot the treasury through inflated contracts, illegal bunkering, import license racketeering and other shady economic deals. Blurring the distinction between the mechanism of the state and the underworld draws attention to the failing nature of the state.

When the play opens, the military regime has just forcefully ejected the inhabitants of Maroko from this Lagos suburb, on the grounds that the place onstitutes a health risk and that it serves as a breeding ground for hoodlums.[1] No alternative provision is made for their accommodation while the demolition is ffected in defiance of judicial intervention. The Maroko dislocation impacts on happenings at the opulent shopping plaza where a group of dwellers of the fringe f urban life – Sanda, Barber, Judge, Trader, Mama Put, Boyko, Shop Worker, Newsvendor and Minstrel – earn their living.

The displacement also coincides with the high profile wedding involving he children of the Sematu and Kingboli families. Preparation for the wedding necessitates that the area of the shopping plaza is cleared of miscreants, but the tuation brings the Area Boys into confrontation with the agents of the military regime. Violence becomes a tool of living, legitimated by the military order. The play ends with a subversion of expectation reminiscent of *The Lion and the Jewel*. Miseyi, the bride, chooses as her groom, Sanda, the king of Area Boys, in place of the rich and influential son of Kingboli. The development creates tension between members of the two families and they have to return to Government House to settle the quarrel. It has, however, set the Area Boys and agents of the state on collision course. Sanda and the group are able to avert the impending disaster, using their wit. Not only do they escape the hands of the law, they set the police against the army in a likely bloody combat of men in uniform.

At the head of the gang of Area Boys is Sanda. They dwell on the fringes of urban life. Sanda is a university graduate who has taken a less desirable job of a shop-front security after roaming the streets for years without employment. However, Sanda brings his education and sharp wit to bear on the job. He also makes available to the community of Area Boys his critical consciousness, anti-establishment disposition and splendid organizing skills. He weaves them into a formidable group able to meet the challenges of existence in a hostile city. These attributes account for his personal victory in marrying Miseyi over the rich son of Kingboli. They also facilitate the victory of the marginalized over the powerful. At the end of the play, the Area Boys outsmart their antagonists in state uniform.

One fascinating aspect of Sanda's portrait is his natural intelligence and vast knowledge of literature and politics which enable him to have an answer to every challenging situation. He is attractive for his intelligence but deplorable as a receiver of stolen goods and a facilitator of burglary and extortion. As the alter ego of the satirist, he contributes to the censure of military autocracy. But he provides a flicker of democratic prospect in a land plagued by authoritarianism through his leadership style, and herein lies his ambivalence: a prodigy of learning tucked in 'a ludicrous store front security cap' (p. 46).

Sanda is well respected in the community of Area Boys. Indeed, he is the King of Area Boys. His influence also extends to the prisoners whose welfare he ensures, apart from teaching them songs. Trader attests his organizational adeptness:

> TRADER: The neighbourhood owe you plenty. Until you come here begin orga nize everybody, we just dey run about like chicken wey no get head. (p. 65)

He is a leader who puts the interests of the community first and is always on hand to rescue members of the community from trouble. Interestingly, Sanda is like Esu Elegbara, the Yoruba trickster god who draws those he likes out of trouble and pushes those he does not favour into disaster (like the rampaging soldiers after the aborted societal wedding).

The recession that follows the oil boom era produced different desperate measures by people to maintain their materialistic tastes nurtured with the ill-managed abundance of oil wealth. Such measures range from the criminal to the outlandishly superstitious. Some people believe that there are certain rituals that when performed, can land them with stupendous wealth. Even when such people are warned that the rituals have dos and don'ts which, if disregarded, would bring incalculable disaster, desperation will still push them to engage in ritual and this may require sacrificing a whole human being or part of the human anatomy. That Sanda stands out of the desperate lot enables him to offer a critique of the vices foisted on the nation by the depressed economy emblematized by the 'get-rich-quick' syndrome.

Mama Put's story recalls Nigeria's experience during the civil war – a needless war precipitated by the gradual descent of the nation from colonial rule into absolutism superintended by fellow blacks. The inescapable conclusion from this narrative is that both the federalists and the secessionists were vicious and acted more like enemies of the people than friends of those they claimed to be liberating. It was a war in which the common people's interests were largely marginal. The forceful displacement of a million people in the Lagos environ Maroko recalls the experience of the civil war and shows the nation as perpetually in crisis, defying the coercive methods of the autocratic state. The Maroko experience, according to Mama Put, was like a war waged by the government against its own citizens.

The military officer who leads the corps that clears Broad Street of miscreants in readiness for the wedding demonstrates the culture of arbitrariness and violence. He justifies the violent eviction of Maroko inhabitants, in spite of a court injunction restraining the government (p. 81). The officer celebrates the primacy of the uniform in governance in the song – 'Don't Touch my Uniform' (pp. 83–4). The uniform is a sacrosanct object that confers on its wearer, limitless powers, rights and privileges. He is insensitive to the rights of others and would not tolerate any opposition or obstacle to the accomplishment of his assignment – clearing the shopping plaza of hoodlums. Hence, he orders that the crowd should be violently displaced and the judge tear-gassed and locked in the booth of his car. The military governor who presides over the aborted high class wedding would not want the quarrel between the two families discussed in the open; hence, he requests that they retire to the state house to iron out their differences. The state house here is the place where corruption is hatched, executed and culprits screened from prosecution; immunized by state power.

The setting, the frontage of the shopping plaza, juxtaposes wealth and poverty, power and powerlessness. It also provides a veritable site for the contestation of power between the military authority and another kind of coercive authority, the Area Boys, who mimic in a more disturbing manner the violent character of the military government.

The operatic method used in the play is also worthy of note. The lyrics of the songs in *The Beatification* are as topical and censorious of arbitrary rule as dialogue and actions. The songs constitute separate performance elements that enrich signification and aesthetic gratification. They are used to ventilate the harshness of repression, corruption, poverty, unemployment, insecurity and instability among other ills. Giving lie to the pretensions and messianic claims of soldiers in power is a vital step toward re-awakening civil society to recover its democratic will.

On the whole, the play shows that absolute rule of the military has foisted on Nigeria, and indeed Africa, a prolonged state of unrest, chaos and stagnation. The condition is so deplorable that Prisoner 2 laments the fate of the people: 'At least, prison get stability. I sorry too much for all these people wey still dey outside. How den dey manage survive, ehn how anybody dey manage?' (p. 70). As implied in the 'Army Conga' song, the ship of the state is simply drifting in the present order of disorder.

King Baabu

With its primary focus on General Sani Abacha's regime in Nigeria, *King Baabu* reviews the second coming of military rule, starting with the preceding eras of General Muhammadu Buhari and General Ibrahim Babangida. Overtly, the play evokes tragic pathos, but this is laced with a bitter satiric indignation against a despotic order in which Nigerians contend with what Soyinka calls 'Abacha's vampiric fangs' (2006: 466). Abacha is depicted as a pervert who harbours a masochistic and banal conception of power. Soyinka also describes him as 'General Sani Abacha; the "butcher of Abuja"' (p. 7), as he charges him with nurturing an agenda – 'the perpetuation of military rule' (p. 28).

Bash is created in the image of 'Giants' in Soyinka's earlier play, *A Play of Giants*. But his monstrosity is so striking that he alone occupies the gallery of ridicule that is Guatuna. What is being celebrated is the hollowness of grandeur in which the despots cloak themselves as signified ironically in the word *baabu* which means 'nothing' or 'lack'. The fabled Guatuna here is close to the fictive Free Republic of Aburiria which provides the setting of Ngugi wa Thiong'o's novel on power politics in Africa, *Wizard of the Crow*.

In a way, the brutal General Basha Bash who later transforms into a 'monarchical democrat' as King Baabu, is a montage of monstrosity in whom one can recognize the despotic leaders who have appropriated Africa's political landscape in the post-independence years. With a leader like Abacha, military rule has lost its allure, even though it held some hope at its inception.

King Baabu was premiered at the National Theatre, Lagos on 6 August 2001. The play echoes in a familiar tone, Alfred Jarry's *Ubu Roi*, a classical precursor of a Twentieth century European theatre form: the theatre of the absurd. The mutual exchange of obscenities, the obsession with power and wealth, as well as the romanticization of food that characterize the relationship between Basha Bash and his vixenish wife Maariya (a thinly veiled reference to Abacha and his wife, Maryam), recall the character traits of Pere Ubu and Mere Ubu in Jarry's model. Basha Bash's blind and ruthless pursuit of his ambition reminds one of Shakespeare's Macbeth while his intellectual vacuity recalls that of Kamini in *A Play of Giants*.

For most of the time when Abacha was in power (1993–98), Soyinka was in exile. But from his outpost, he launched a relentless attack against Abacha's reign of terror and looting. In Soyinka's words:

> We are not dealing here even with a specie of civilized villain.
> In Abacha's case, there is nothing but emptiness (emphasis added).
> Just cruelty, sadism, power lust totally disproportionate to his
> intellectual capacities. He is nothing, just a superstitious and
> sadistic being. (1994: 3)

The comment above sums up the portrait of Basha Bash in *King Baabu*. He is shown as the physical embodiment of savagery and a personification of evil. Kpoki reinforces this image when he remarks about Baabu: 'Sometimes I wonder whether we're dealing with a human being or the Devil incarnate' (p. 86).

The idea of emptiness is captured paradoxically in the nothingness of *King Baabu*. He makes up for his slender intellectual capacities with his big barrel stomach and huge appetite for food. Shoki calls him a 'disgusting barrel of lard' (p. 70). The weird crown he wears (a conical brass fruit bowl) says much about the banality and hollowness of this monstrous monarch.

The play celebrates the disastrous end of a tyrant. The death elicits a kind of catharsis, with Guatuna ridden of a man who has done so much to endanger its survival, even when he claims to be a messiah. Here, tyranny is consumed by its own (il)logic of wantonness and arbitrariness. Under King Baabu, all aspects of governance lose their essence and allure. Concepts like democracy, freedom, accountability, justice, family values, trade unionism, religion, and monarchy are greatly devalued. His metamorphosis into a 'democratic monarch' notwithstanding, his sadistic acts never abate, just as corruption and superstition reign supreme. Like Baabu's royal crown after his fall at the battle front, democratic ideals under the military have become 'squashed and twisted and crooked' (72). His catastrophic end, therefore, comes like that of the trickster in the traditional African folktale who overreaches himself and is consumed by his own greed. His son, Biibabae (like his father) is an undisputed heir to his father's viciousness. He applies the electric shock to a suspected rebel and his yell of discomfort gives music to the ears of the royal couple. His father 'hops up and down in manic excitement' (p. 83).

Apart from King Baabu, the common people who often shift positions do not escape the barb of Soyinka's satire. They are guilty of short memories or 'collective amnesia'. It is this collective amnesia that makes them to readily accept any regime that comes to power. The people are like the Roman plebeians in Shakespeare's

Julius Caesar and *Coriolanus* who change their opinions like the weather vane that is blown by the wind. At the sight of money and food, they change their denunciation of King Baabu to approbation. Through the crowd, Soyinka parodies the general populace in reality. Their acquiescence, amnesia, cynical resignation, lethargy, ignorance, gullibility and sometimes, greed are weaknesses that often create an enabling environment for the festering of tyranny.

In Basha Bash and Maariya, the playwright creates a couple bound by greed and obscenity. Both are perverts and masochists, who enjoy inflicting pains on others. Basha is an experienced coup plotter who has installed several regimes. Maariya is an ambitious woman who covets power. To Basha, his wife is 'an early morning pestilence on a man's peace', a 'she cow' (p. 6). To Maariya, he is a 'goat-fucker from the winds of wilderness', a 'dithering apostate', a 'voracious virago (p. 77). Baabu's grotesquery is evident not only in the way he freely exchanges insult with Maariya, but also in the way he describes violent and blood-curdling situations with relish. An example is the murder of the former Head of State, General Uzi.

Basha, a thinly-veiled reference to Abacha, is presented as an under-developed adult, judging from his diction. His limited vocabulary sometimes hinders effective communication and that impels him to violence in response to dissent. In terms of diction, Soyinka uses pun, paradox, irony and symbolism in *King Baabu*. He explores dual meanings implied in a word and stretches their potentials for signification. Dual meanings enable him to juxtapose the fictional and the actual realities, revealing in the process a lack of correspondence between the actual and what ought to be represented in the stage presentation. These rhetorical elements also lend humour to the overall satiric aesthetics. For instance, Shoki, using innuendo, says that Basha is somewhere 'milking the cow of opportunity' (p. 33), and that accounts for his absence. Basha too extends the meaning of this phrase further:

> But I think as long as he think I give him banking cow to milk, he remaining loyal. Trouble begin when he see that I intend to milk banking cow myself. Ah national cow in fact. No room under this go'ment for any sacred cow. (p. 37)

'Sacred cow' has introduced a different but related element to the subject. It implies that Basha is determined to be impartial and firm. But it also hints at his 'not to be contested' supremacy and dominance. Consequently one can appreciate the concept of probity, accountability, openness and mass participation in Baabu's democracy. The monarch holds court and eats in the 'open balcony…where everybody can watch' (p. 56). He demands that bank chiefs should sign 'open cheques' and order that those who do not comply be pushed into an 'open pit' as punishment. He advises the tenant who is dislodged from his house by the landlord to continue to live with his family in the 'open air':

> BAABU: See? Government policy already working. This now democracy, open society. You see my office here, also in the open. When everybody begin work, eat, sleep and shit and fuck in the open, then we know we already reach the promised land. (p. 56)

The citizens of Batwere who vote in a mayor in an election without the prior consent of King Baabu are punished with amputation. They have their 'hands' chopped off for 'taking law into own hands' (p. 100). Here, a familiar expression – 'taking the law into one's own hands' is rendered in a literal sense that takes it out of its familiar context through deliberate distortion and pun. Added to this is the use of euphemism to lessen the harshness of despotism. For example, Basha Bash calls the coup that brings him into power as 'a change of command' (p. 35) rather than being a forceful takeover of power and a betrayal of trust.

The characters of DOPE, RENT and ROUT, all civilian collaborators who prop up dictatorship by their acts of sycophancy, are vital to the satiric message of the play. They represent the religious institution, royalty and labour unionism available to buy legitimacy for military autocrats or civilians who pervert democracy through questionable elections. They are always there to court power, with Uzi, Rajinda, Potipoo, Basha and back to Potipoo.

The acronyms – SCAR, RENT, DOPE and ROUT – are noteworthy. Just as the military ruling body, the Supreme Council for Advance Redemption (SCAR) eaves indelible traces of repression on the polity, Royal Estates Nominal and Traditional (RENT) points to traditional rulers as always supporting and finding accommodation in any political dispensation, colonial, civilian or military to foist on the people, a 'rentier' state. They live on 'rents', tributes and taxes collected from their subjects. The Divine Order of Prelates Ecumenical (DOPE) shows the religious organizations to be a kind of opium, doping the critical consciousness of he people. In Marxist thought, religion is seen as the opium of the masses, which tands between them and a materialist understanding of the universe. Religion in this dramatic context screens the people from apprehending the insidious workings of tyranny. The labour movement represented by the Recognized and Organized Unio n of all Trades (ROUT) is compromised and it is part of the litist conspiracy that facilitates the ascendancy of absolute rule. Rather than being the critical voice of the working people, ROUT is incorporated into the organs of the corrupt state, working to 'rout' the people in their struggle for good overnance.

Overall, Soyinka in *King Baabu* stresses the betrayal of expectation by the military as regards the restoration of people's rule. As Tikim, puts it, 'Democracy is about to be midwived by the military. It is an awesome, historical, and monumental undertaking' (p. 18). But events under King Baabu subvert this expectation as Guatuna is saddled with venomous tyranny masquerading as 're-inventing the state'.

One element of craft common to the three plays is irony. It manifests in the setting, conflicts and characterization. The device reflects how far removed the polity is from the democratic destination towards which the ruling elites claim to be heading. In terms of stage rhetoric, wit, pun and word associations are employed to register the tenuous gap between democracy and dictatorship in the satirised polity.

Concluding Remarks

Soyinka stands out among African writers for his consistent engagement with the political history of the continent through literature. This has become more pronounced since the second coming of military dictatorship in Nigeria (1983–99), which coincided with a period of global disenchantment with, and disengagement from, autocratic rule, especially in Africa. It is pleasing to note that self-perpetuating absolutist regimes reduced on the continent in the last two decades of the 20th century. The trend has continued to date, the latest berth of the gale being Egypt, Tunisia, Côte d'Ivoire and Libya. Perhaps Cameroon, Burkina Faso and Uganda may not be too far away from the wild wind. Abuse of human rights, disregard for due process, manipulation of constitutions for sectarian purposes and self-perpetuation in office are still being experienced in these and other countries.

In spite of the feeble will that often attends their pronouncements, intra-continental organisations such as the African Union (AU), the Economic Community of West African States (ECOWAS), and *Communauté Economique et Monitaire des Etats de l'Afrique Centrale* (CEMAC) have resolved against undemocratic means of accessing power among member states. This is a significant step, but it should be followed by a programme of cleansing the culture of impunity. Psychic reconditioning is quite fundamental to progress and development in the new century, more than ever before. Although democratic principles and practices are never monolithic in construction, neither are the constituents ever complete and sealed; they are open to local imperatives. But what we should not accept and accommodate is the subordination of the will of the majority to that of the powerful and privileged few as often happens in autocratic regimes.[2] The exposition of this among other aberrations is guaranteed in Soyinka's dramaturgy as the foregoing analyses of The Beatification of Area Boy and King Baabu have shown. While capturing the raison d'être of Soyinka's writing, this essay demonstrates how absolute rule in different forms has impeded democratic governance and development on the African continent, especially in Nigeria, in the post-independent years.

In many instances, military interventions in politics have been justified, citing collapse of the rule of law, economic mismanagement and political instability. Soldiers too often seek legitimacy from the people, using the promise to 'restor democracy', however indefinite the time plan. But such attempts often fail because of the authoritarian ethos built into the transition programmes. Soyinka captures the contradictions inherent in this historical reality through characterization, setting and patterns of conflict in the two plays discussed above. He creates hollow characters who suffer delusions of grandeur in his attempt to pillory absolute rule. Thus, the audience is confronted with images of military (mis) rule, an important factor in understanding the causes of underdevelopment and instability in post-independent Africa. Generally, there is a close affinity between the tenor of politics and artistic trends in Soyinka's dramaturgy. His plays serve as another platform for his critical interventions in the dilemma of the postcolony. This is worthy of closer attention in any serious effort by intellectuals to come to terms with the African predicament in the unfolding century.

One notes the cynicism that characterizes the critical realistic portrayal of the myriad of problems confronting the continent in Soyinka's plays. However, beyond the cynicism is an indication that authoritarian modes of governance do not subsist for long. The seed of the death of despotism is usually sown at its inception. The victory of the Area Boys in *The Beatification* and the death of King Baabu point to the limits of tyranny.

When and where genuinely practised, democracy holds the key to sustainable development. The success of democracy is predicated on a sufficient knowledge of the inadequacies of the immediate past and present. What becomes so imperative here is a relentless engagement through all modes of socio-cultural expressions, including drama, with the fate of the state. Soyinka contends that the culture of coercion reminiscent of the military era must be eradicated, just as the populace must purge itself of the 'needless' fear of the man in the military uniform. 'Civic will' needs to be re-invigorated in order to achieve a balance or regulate the constitution and the laws. In his words, democracy is 'a social platform…better still, a trampoline – but balanced on three legs: Constitution, Law and Civic will'. He further submits that at the moment:

> The Constitution is pot-holed. The Temple of Justice (Law) is sullied. And Civic Will? Destabilized. Ultimately nonetheless, that last (Civic will) remains – for the most obvious reasons – the enduring repository of collective, inclusive responsibilities, catalysts also in motions to sustain the stability of the democratic platform, turning it into a steady plane, so it does not bounce society up and down as on its present trampoline". (2011)

Besides, there should also be a clear contract between the people and the state or between the rulers and the ruled. As Tansi puts it, 'the absence of a clear social contract between the people and its leaders dooms the latter to infantilization. It is only through the exercise of responsibility that one is human. The refusal to entrust the people with responsibility condemns our continent to bring up the rear on the chess board of the future' (2007: 273).

Africa in the twenty-first century should also ensure that the culture of impunity imposed in the authoritarian past is made a permanent non-factor in the emerging democracy. In fact, both the rampaging soldiers and the acquiescing populace must undergo a holistic psychological re-birth towards the de-militarization of the polity. The commoditization of power whereby, even in a civilian dispensation, power is only accessed by a few wealthy citizens who exercise it in pursuit of personal benefits and narrow group interests should also be discouraged. Soyinka's plays, informed about the political realities of contemporary Africa, constitute a means of stock-taking or re-evaluation towards developing alternative societies far removed from the aberrant ones satirized on the stage. One remedy constantly on offer in his theatre is a deliberate devaluation of tyranny and tyrants, rendering both as thoroughly stained as Kongi and as irredeemably repulsive as King Baabu. Therefore, it is not too late, yet, for Africa to 'set forth' on the path of truly democratic governance towards-people centred development at the 'dawn' of another decade in the twenty-first century.

Notes

1. Lagos state military government under Colonel Raji Rasaki effected the demolition of Maroko, a Lagos suburb, in 1990.
2. See interview with Soyinka in *The News Magazine,* Lagos, 28 November 1994.

References

Adeoti, Gbemisola, 2006. 'Post Aminian Fantasia: Despots, Democrats and Othe[r] Mutations in Soyinka's Recent Drama', in Gbemisola Adeoti and Mabe[l] Evwierhoma, eds, *After the Nobel Prize: Reflections on African Literature, Governanc[e] and Development*, Lagos: Association of Nigerian Authors.

Davidson, Basil, 1992, *The Blackman's Burden: Africa and the Curse of the Nation State*, New York: Times Book.

Diamond, Larry et al., eds, 1988, *Democracy in Developing Countries: Africa (Vol. II)*, Colorado: Lynne Rienner Publishers.

Kein, George Klay, and Agbese, Pita Ogaba, eds, 2008, *The State in Africa: Issues an[d] Perspectives*, Ibadan: Kraft Books Limited.

Oloruntimehin, Olatunji, 2007, *Culture and Democracy*, Lagos: CBAAC Occasiona[l] Monograph, No. 5.

Osofisan, Femi, 1998, *Playing Dangerously: Drama at the Frontiers of Terror in a 'Postcolonia[l]' State*, Inaugural Lecture, Ibadan: University of Ibadan.

Soyinka, Wole, 1986, 'This Past Must Address Its Present', Nobel Lecture, Stockholm, 8 December.

Soyinka, Wole, 1994. 'Kongi's Outrage', *The News Magazine*, Lagos, 19 December.

Soyinka, Wole, 1995, *The Beatification of Area Boy: A Lagosian Kaleidoscope*, Ibadan: Spectrum Books.
Soyinka, Wole, 1996, 'Toward a Sustainable Vision of Nigeria'. An address delivered at the Summit for Democracy in Oslow, Norway, 3 March.
Soyinka, Wole, 2002, *King Baabu*, London: Methuen.
Soyinka, Wole, 2006, *You Must Set forth at Dawn*, Ibadan: Bookcraft.
Soyinka, Wole, 2011, 'Teetering on the Democratic Trampoline', key note address delivered at the Conference of the Nigerian Bar Association (NBA), Port Harcourt, Nigeria, August.
Tansi, Sony Labou, 2007, 'An Open Letter to Africans c/o The Punic One-Party State',in Tejumola Olaniyan and Ato Quayson, eds, *African Literature: An Anthology of Criticism and Theory*, Malden, USA: Blackwell Publishing.
wa Thiong'o, Ngugi, 2007, *Wizard of the Crow*, Lagos: Farafina.

3

A Critical Discourse Evaluation of Decolonisation and Democratisation: Issues in Africa as Exemplified in Soyinka's Non-fictional Texts

Henry Hunjo

Introduction

Africans deserve quality of life. By this we mean what is generally referred to as good living conditions, where social provisions that make human beings enjoy existence are available in adequate supply. These provisions and their constant supply have been seen to be the responsibility of governments of African states. Africa, therefore, deserves leaders whose goals must necessarily include the consideration that human beings deserve growth and improved living conditions in all ramifications. Attention must be given to health, economy, development (infrastructural, physical, social and mental), water resources, food security and social security. African nations, after independence, have had to contend with problems of development and good governance (Giddens 2006:406). The relics of colonisation, hospitals, pipe-borne water, electricity, the civil service, the military, the police and other social agents and functionaries, point to the fact that certain ideas supported the establishment of social institutions to cater for the human conditions of the colonial citizens. Therefore, one would expect the sustenance of these structures and institutions with the goal of further improving lives of Africans. At independence, most African nations could afford basic amenities. But, ten years after, the dreams of development began to give way to despondency.

The reality today is that many African nations have failed to be fully independent after the departure of the colonial administrators. Some people see this failure as a manifestation of selfishness on the part of affluent leaders, believing that access to European culture and Western civilisation should have influenced governance towards achieving genuine development. They argue further that if the exposure that the leaders have had through Western education and travels to Europe had been meaningful, then, the experiences garnered from constant visits to Europe and America should have impacted on the judgement of the leaders to make them think of what could be done in the ex-colonies they now rule. Africans have certain expectations which ought to have been fulfilled by their leaders, but which are yet to be met especially those that should have ensured true liberation and democratisation of the polity. There is a yearning on the continent for representative democracy and wide discontent with dictatorship as demonstrated in the recent political upheavals in North Africa.

Theory and Methods of Post-colonialism

Many African nations recently celebrated their fifty years of independence. This implies that fifty years after colonial rule is an adequate and appropriate time for stock-taking. Little wonder, then, thinking within the confines of post-colonial theory, one is confronted with the problems associated with the gulf between the centre and the periphery. The distinction between the centre and the periphery remains one of the agitating theoretical issues in post-colonial studies. The choice of post-colonialism as a theoretical plank upon which arguments in this essay are anchored is deliberate. The theory is useful in the attempt to develop an interdisciplinary methodology of text analysis in the field of Critical Discourse Analysis. While this is concerned primarily with the relationship between language and society and how language is used to construct social realities in texts, post-colonial theory demands that the analyst should identify socially situated texts for the purpose of discovering salient ideologies.

The study of Wole Soyinka's non-fictional texts to identify the templates of political thinking of post-colonial African leaders is incomplete without an understanding the nature of the centre and the periphery before and after independence. One of the salient assumptions in Soyinka's writings is that African leaders have their minds tutored to deliberately (this may be a hard concept to prove) engender political leadership devoid of development concepts. In this chapter we have adopted methods of text analysis found in the critical discourse analysis developed by Norman Fairclough (1989) and Teun van Dijk (1996). The choice of these models of critical discourse has been informed by some aspects of their work that could be fused together for the purpose of solving specific problems found in the subject under study. Fairclough's (1989) idea of Members' Resources (MR) agrees with van Dijk's (1996) concept of Long Term Memory (LTM). Fairclough's concept is deeply rooted in the provisions of social theories and their effects on tex description, production and consumption. On the other hand, van Dijk's concept relies on knowledge advancement in cognitive psychology and its effects on text. The deployment of aspects of these concepts to analyse text is relevant to understanding post-colonial thinking within the context of language used to represent a set of specific social ideas. These social ideas determine what constitutes the reactions behind some social actions that can explain why African leaders could not evolve strategies of governance comparable to what obtains in many developed nations of Europe and America. We need a combination of information from socially-related concepts and cognitive psychology to explain the attitudes of African leaders as described by Soyinka. This idea is at the core of my perception of the relationship between the centre and the periphery.

During the colonial era in African states, it was clear that the centre was made up of the colonial administrators representing the colonising powers of Europe. Governance was a product of the colonial home government policies. Decisions about governance were taken by colonial rulers, using the British or French system of government. In the British colonies, for instance, the system operated was Indirect Rule. African traditional rulers were used to enforce British laws in the colonies. These African leaders then were members of the peripheral class with their long term memories partly rooted in their African social cultural backgrounds and the rest in the newly acquired colonial ways. The situation was such that the governed that constituted the periphery were made up of traditional African leaders and their subjects. If we exclude the colonial leaders from the picture, what we had were two classes: the centre (African traditional ruling councils) and the periphery (the subjects). Now, with the colonial masters in the picture, we had a composite of two classes: the centre (colonial masters) and the periphery (African traditional ruling councils and their subjects).

Shortly after the Second World War, nationalist movements and a new set of African leaders emerged. These were the educated elite who struggled to take over power from the colonial masters. Gradually, as independence approached, the centre and the periphery began to change identity. With independence, the responsibility of leadership devolved to educated African leaders. The centre was no longer occupied by the colonial masters but by educated Africans. The periphery was and it is still made up of the subjects.

As stated earlier, colonial governments provided amenities to 'the natives' during the colonial era. Governance, then, addressed the welfare of the citizens. Five decades after the independence of many African nations, problems of leadership remain fundamental. This compels one to ask: of what pyschological stock are the post-colonial African leaders made? This question is addressed in this chapter through an interrogation of Soyinka's non-fictional writings. Soyinka has trenchantly shown that the decolonisation and democratisation project in Africa will not yield much unless African leaders change and provide a clear vision of political leadership.

The Non-fictional Writings of Soyinka

The writings of Wole Soyinka have always been identified with revolt against existing political systems (Adeniran 1994: 50). Linguists and literary scholars have engaged with his works, trying to 'demystify' his language (Osakwe 1992; Adejare 1992; Adeniran 1994; Ogunsiji 2001). What is common to many of these critical works is the comment on the 'turgidity' of his linguistic structures and the deployment of uncommon imagery to represent thoughts on matters of political import in search of social change. Soyinka's competence in the use of English has never been in contention, but his struggles and revolts are constant thematic issues requiring the attention of text analysts (Ogunsiji 2001).

Soyinka's writings depict him as a political maverick. His beliefs and actions in the realm of politics are somewhat iconoclastic. He believes in humanism and promotes the pursuit of human dignity from that perspective. To him, politics should be about improving the lot of humankind such that happiness, provisions of social amenities, peace of mind, sound health and general wellbeing become the necessary dividends of good governance. The improvement of the human condition, therefore, is the cardinal goal of genuine democracy. How this composite feature of democracy is represented in his writings is the central focus of the chapter. This exercise requires viewing a text as a site for social interaction where participants engage in activities that are intertwined at various social levels.

Soyinka's role in setting up resistance machinery, the Third Force, during the civil war (Jeyifo 2004:7), was a response to the desire to confront anti-democratic policies of the Nigerian political class. As an academic, Soyinka's radicalism is not confined to the classroom. Rather, he is constantly confronted with the responsibility of leading protests and raising the consciousness of his audience towards achieving true liberation for the downtrodden. Analysing Soyinka's texts is premised on the assumption that the growth process of the writer from childhood to adulthood determines the kind of messages embedded in the texts selected for analysis here. One of the ways to understand a writer's production strategy is to investigate his socio-cultural background and how that leads to self-description and self-identity. Reflexivity from this perspective helps the reader to see the reason behind the writer's choice of genre, register, topic of discourse (field), medium of communication (mode) and other relevant factors (Fairclough 1995:138; Gee 1999:40; Dijk 2002:112).

As an illustration, this chapter discusses Soyinka's recent memoir, *You Must Set Forth at Dawn*. One thing that comes to the fore is the gulf between the aspirations of the citizens and the expectations of the ruling elite in many countries of Africa. The memoir, published in 2006, is a detailed account of Soyinka's personal experiences in the politics and life of Nigeria. Though the book is about Nigeria, it contains experiences that are common to other parts of the continent

Attention is paid to the lexical constructs that depict the behaviours of politicians. The text discusses politics, democracy, violence, racism, activism, international politics and intellectualism, culture and religion and humanism.

Lexical Indexicalisation of Political Actors

Lexical indexicalisation of political actors in text is a discourse practice that enables text producers to construct characters' identities to reflect mental constructs that text consumers need to deploy as text interpretation cues to detect not just the identity of a character but what powers actions. This cannot be done without the knowledge of the function of the subconscious and how that unconsciously influences habits of individuals or groups in some contexts. Bourdieu has used the term *habitus* to describe some sort of unconscious mechanistic manifestation of some habits in social context (Robbins 2000:26–7) and his explanation is close to what we mean here. Soyinka's goal of drawing attention to some of the reasons African nations are yet to achieve development motivates him to coin some lexical items that indexicalise political actors of the independent era as unfit for the administration of the newly independent states. Using two samples from *You Must Set Forth At Dawn* (SFD in subsequent references), this chapter examines some of these lexical items and identifies the relationship between the lexical meaning of the expressions and, how in political contexts, they account for the prevalence in Africa of tyranny, economic profligacy, corruption and other anti-development factors.

Forces militating against decolonisation and democratisation are products of the conditioning found in the beliefs of African politicians. The conditioning operates against the will of the politicians themselves. Past African leaders have never come up with any explanation to defend their behaviours while in power, to justify their inability to work for the development of their nations to be on a par with highly developed nations of the world. Somehow, the pre-independence politicians of Africa were not sure of where to direct their patriotism. Soyinka paints the picture clearly:

> The nationalists, the first generation of elected leaders and legislators of our semi-independent nation had begun to visit Great Britain in droves. We watched their self-preening, their ostentatious spending, their cultivated condescension, even disdain towards the people they were supposed to represent… Most of the time however, as we ran eagerly to welcome the protagonists of the African Renaissance, we were bombarded by utterances that identified only flamboyant replacements of the old colonial order, not transforming agents not even empathising participants in a process of liberation. (SFD, p. 48)

The excerpt is an example of an account of the nature of the conduct of pre-independence politicians. The failure of politicians to attend to the human needs of their subjects bred tyranny. Tyranny is a system of government in which the tyrant thinks only of his personal interest and of those close to him. In the excerpt above, politicians of the pre-independence era are depicted as people who did not have the interests of the citizens and the nation at heart. Being self-centred, they lavish state funds on personal interests. Soyinka constructs a context that helps us to see that there was no genuine preparation for the independent state, nor for the indoctrination of the emerging political leaders to consider state interest first before personal interest. The discovery here is that Soyinka's construction of the characters of the first generation of politicians depicts these leaders as exhibiting traits of tyranny.

The representation of tyranny in Soyinka's political discourse reveals deeper understanding of the way the foundation of tyranny was laid at the time when African nations attained the status of self-rule in the late 1950s and 1960s. The prevalence of tyranny in many African nations in the decade after independence can, therefore, be attributed to the anti-democratic practices of the early nationalists. The following lexical items in the quotation above indexicalise the facts:

> 'self-preening'
> 'ostentatious spending'
> 'cultivated condescension'
> 'disdain'

These lexical items describe the attitude the politicians show and that the leaders who took over from the colonial administrators were concerned more with their personal interests, especially their identities. The lexical items raise questions of the role of leaders as state builders versus the need to attend to their self-esteem needs as individuals. The worry then is to ascertain whether the politicians were state builders or self-builders.

The idea that the early Nigerian political leaders were trained by the British is instantiated in the excerpt. The sentence, 'The nationalists, the first generation of elected leaders and legislators of our semi-independent nation had begun to visit Great Britain in droves', points to that reality, but Soyinka is quick to point out that the visit to Britain then lacked orderliness as depicted by the prepositional group 'in droves'. The disorderliness also presented opportunities for the politicians to exhibit their capacity for profligacy. The critical discourse value of the instance of difference in political vision enacted in this excerpt demonstrates the qualities of the pre-independence politicians and their anti-decolonisation actions.

The major ideology revealed in this text is that a tyrannical government is constituted by people who understand the meaning and dynamics of power, but prefer it be exercised by a few instead of the majority. These political actors are ironically, referred to in the text as 'the protagonists of African Renaissance'. The idea of renaissance is one of the expectations of the citizens of the newly emancipated nation. The newly elected leaders are seen as to be protagonists, meaning that it the new democratic order that was awaited in the late 1950s, leaders were supposed to be supporters of representative governance. The account in Soyinka's political discourse indicates that the reverse was the case as the politicians are reported to engage in 'utterances that identified only flamboyant replacement of the old colonial order, not transforming agents, not even empathising participants in a process of liberation'. The salient ideology here is that inherent in the mental composition of the politicians: a fragment of enslaving strategy taken from the orientation provided by the British colonial masters to show that the emerging centre would not really be sensitive to the welfare needs of the peripheral class.

The excerpt presents an interaction within an on-going democratisation process that requires the entrenchment of transformation from a detested colonial rule to free and independent governance; a democratic republic where people freely choose their leaders. Therefore, reference to political leaders as 'elected legislators' indicates that democracy was the preferred system of government when Nigeria attained independence in 1960. The use of the expression, 'only flamboyant replacement of the old colonial order', describes the fact that the British colonial masters manipulated the handover of political leadership to favour their stooges in order to perpetuate colonial hegemony. That is why the attitude of the political leaders when they got to Britain did not show any sense of commitment to the enthronement of a free and liberal democracy. The statement that reveals tyrannical foundation is the last part of the sentence, 'not even the empathising participants in a process of liberation'. The psycho-social quality that ensures inclusion as an element of liberal democracy is empathy. The lack of empathy in the elected politicians and their manner of leading a life of debauchery concluded the laying of the foundation for tyranny in post-colonial governance. In this order, the feelings and views of the governed would not matter.

As indicated earlier, the politicians were prone to profligacy, a vice that was curiously condoned by the British colonialists. Soyinka puts it in these words:

> Some turned students into pimps, either for immediate rewards, or in return for influence in obtaining or extending scholarships. Visiting politicians financed lavished parties for one sole purpose – to bring on the girls! They appeared to have only one ambition on the brain – to sleep with a white woman. For that privilege, in addition to discarding the dignity of their position, they would pay more than the equivalent of our monthly student allowances. We watched them heap unbelievable gifts on virtual prostitutes, among whom both British and continental students could be counted. (SFD, p. 48)

Soyinka's main aim in depicting the activities of Nigeria's ruling elite at independence is to deepen readers' understanding of the sources of tyranny. His self-indexicalisation in the narration as an observer-participant in the events is marked by the use of the first person plural pronoun, 'we', in all contexts concerning the activities of Nigerian students and politicians of the early self-rule era. 'We' refers to the foreign students in England in the 1950s. These students were drawn from different African countries and their main concern was to acquire higher education in order to return to their respective nations to participate in the 'transformation' of their newly independent states into truly democratic states. The experiences narrated in the extract above shows that the readers should pay attention to the characters of leaders applying the cognitive knowledge of the expected behavioural patterns of genuine leaders.

Leadership in democracy ought to be grounded in the social development needs of the governed. Soyinka's description of the public attitudes of the leaders of the 1950s reveals lexical representation of facts that are characteristic of tyrants. The expression, 'some turned students into pimps and visiting politicians financed lavish parties', reveals the profligate attitudes of the politicians. The differences between the lexical content of the word, 'student', and 'pimps' found in the relational process clause – 'Some turned students into pimps' – foregrounds the hedonistic foundation of many activities of Nigerian leaders of the independence era. Soyinka shows that these leaders lacked a clear-cut ideological direction for the re-creation of a post-colonial order that would lead to the emergence of a truly liberated and independent state in which liberal democracy and social development would thrive. Lexical analysis has drawn attention to the preliminary symptoms of tyranny in the political leaders of Nigeria before actual independence in 1960. It is noteworthy that some African leaders in history manifested elements of hedonism and tyranny in their personal lives: Mobutu Sese Seko, Emperor Jean-Bedel Bokassa, Gnassingbe Eyadema, Sani Abacha, Hosni Mubarak and so on.

Conclusion

It has been established that the centre of African nations since independence, remains attached to the colonial centre. The consequences of this are the doomed periphery destined to be poor in the midst of plenty. The analysis of lexical items above shows that as at the time of independence, the political elites were not prepared to confront the challenges of political liberation and socio-economic growth. Many years of colonialism robbed African nations of their right to ownership of economic resources. Colonial administrative offices were vacant, but control over trade and commerce was still retained by the colonisers as a result of the unpatriotic attitudes of members of the ruling elite. By the 1960s when the nationalists were celebrating the attainment of independence, little did they know that they carried with them beliefs that were enshrined in the conditioning programme designed by the colonial government to ensure the continuation of the colonialists' interest, despite self-rule. Before independence, resource control had been taken over without the consent of the African masses. Bond (2006:2) sees this as looting and describes the situation thus:

> … remind ourselves of the historical legacy of a continent looted: trade by force dating back centuries; slavery that uprooted and dispossessed around 12 million Africans; lan

> grabs; vicious taxation schemes; precious metals spirited away; the appropriation of antiquities to the British Museum and other trophy rooms; the 19th-century emergence of racist ideologies to justify colonialism; the 1884–5 carve-up of Africa, in a Berlin negotiating room, into dysfunctional territories; the construction of settler-colonial and extractive-colonial systems – of which apartheid, the German occupation of Namibia, the Portuguese colonies and King Leopold's Belgian Congo were perhaps only the blatant – often based upon tearing black migrants workers from rural areas (leaving women with vastly increased responsibilities as a consequence); Cold War battlegrounds – proxies for US/USSR conflicts – filled with millions of corpses; other wars catalysed by mineral searches and offshoot violence such as witnessed in blood diamonds and coltan (Colombo-tantelite, a crucial component of cell phones and computer chips); poacher-stripped swathes of East, Central and Southern Africa now devoid of rhinos and elephants whose ivory became ornamental material or aphrodisiac in the Middle East and East Asia; societies used as guinea pigs in the latest corporate pharmaceutical test ... and the list could continue.

Bond's long list here excludes the fact that the new African leaders took note of the looted items before embarking on the administration of the newly independent states. Today, Africa is one of the continents where third world countries abound (Millet and Toussaint 2004:1).

In concluding this chapter, it needs to be stated that African leaders must have their philosophy of leadership changed. The change must be in a direction that puts them in a vantage position where they can resist, at all times, the traps of perpetual poverty and underdevelopment set by The World Bank, IMF and the Paris Club. Findings from social research have indicated that developed nations are responsible for the poverty of Africa because African leaders themselves allow this to happen. Young (2003:134) declares that 'some of the poverty, or at least some suffering, of the people of the non-western world is also the direct result of the actions of their own government' because they fall easy prey to the overtures of the lending agencies of the developed world in order to be politically subservient. It is a continuation of colonialism. Asian countries that have refused conditionalities of such agencies have become successful economic powers. Malaysia, according to Millet and Toussaint (2004:71), 'refused any agreement with the IMF in 1997–98, protected its domestic market and, after the crisis had broken out, took strict control of capital flows and exchange, and the government spent money on giving new impetus to production'. Evidence of Malaysia's economic resurgence is numerous and in the varieties of goods they export to African countries. Until African leaders, too, review the financial aid from these agencies, there may not be true independence (Millet and Toussaint 2004:72). This also requires African leaders to resist the temptation to loot their nations' treasury and stash the loot away in foreign vaults. That can only further enrich already developed countries while impoverishing their own nations and citizens. Instead, they should encourage agriculture and local industries in order to boost production rather than consumption.

References

Adejare, O., 1992, *Language and Style in Soyinka: A Systemic Textlinguistic Study of a Literary Idiolect*, Ibadan: Heinemann Educational Books.

Adeniran, Tunde, 1994, *The Politics of Wole Soyinka,* Ibadan: Fountain Publications.

Bond, P., 2006, *Looting Africa*, London: Zed Books.

Fairclough, N., 1989, *Language and Power,* Essex: Pearson Education Limited.

Bond, P., 2006, *1995, Critical Discourse Analysis: The Critical Study of Language*, London: Longman.

Gee, J. P., 1999, *An Introduction to Discourse Analysis: Theory and Method,* London: Routledge.

Giddens, A., 2006, *Sociology,* Cambridge: Polity Press.

Jeyifo, B., 2004, *Wole Soyinka,* Cambridge: Cambridge University Press.

Millet, D. and Toussaint, E., 2004, *Who Owes Who? 50 Questions about World Debt,* London: Zed Books.

Ogunsiji, A., 2001, 'Decoding Soyinka's Faction: A Linguistic Stylistic Study', PhD thesis, University of Ibadan.

Osakwe, M. I., 1992, 'The Language of Wole Soyinka's Poetry: A Diatype of English', unpublished PhD thesis, University of Ibadan.

Robbins, D., 2000, *Bourdieu and Culture,* London: Sage Publications.

Soyinka, Wole, 2006, *You Must Set Forth at Dawn*, Ibadan: Bookcraft.

van Dijk, T.A., 1996, 'Discourse, Power and Access', in C.R. Caldas-Coulthard and M. Coulthard, eds, *Texts and Practices: Readings in Critical Discourse Analysis*, London: Routledge.

van Dijk, T.A., 2002, 'Discourse, context and cognition', *Discourse studies* 8(1): 159-77.

Young, R. J. C., 2003, *Post-colonialism: A Very Short Introduction,* Oxford: Oxford University Press.

4

Power, Artistic Agency and Poetic Discourse: Poetry as Cultural Critique in Africa

Sule E. Egya

Introduction

Without doubt, literature, especially imaginative writing, played a vital role in the struggles that gave rise to the wave of independence in the 1960s in Africa. Those often regarded as the first generation of African poets in European languages (Léopold Sédar Senghor, Wole Soyinka, Christopher Okigbo, David Diop, Birago Diop and Okot p'Bitek) approached imaginative writing in the 1950s and 1960s with a strong sense of instrumentalism, the social moorings of their works tending towards a counter-narrative. Their works essentially challenged in various ways the Western epistemological system that undermined the very humanity of Africans. Since then, African poetry in foreign and indigenous languages has continued to concern itself with historical events, mostly critiquing socio-political and cultural problems, articulating the travails and triumphs of the common people under oppressive regimes – civilian or military – across the continent. This is evident in the works of Niyi Osundare, Tanure Ojaide, Jack Mapanje and Kofi Anyidoho, among others, who emerged in the 1980s.

The central argument in this chapter is that while new poetic voices continue to emerge on the African literary scene, poetry in Africa, even in the twenty-first century, continues to historicise and critique cultural, social and political challenges which have persistently troubled the continent since independence. While attempting a materialist reading of selected poems published in this century, the essay contends that emerging African poets, like other writers, artists, progressive intellectuals and activists, are concerned about the seemingly bleak state of the continent, and are participating, through their engaged poetry, in the construction of an alternative vision.

Poetry prides itself as the prime example of linguistic unorthodoxy. It has the tendency to enshroud familiar things with an unfamiliar expression. Poetry seeks not to be a medium for expressing views on issues but a performance of words, a staging of artistic craft, often for sheer aesthetic values. At least, this seems to be the conception of poetry handed down to African literati and intellectuals, a conception formulated by Euro-American modernism. But as with the colonial languages, especially the English language, poetry has come to acquire a feature rather distinct in the hands of African poets. While it continues to retain its attribute as an art form that most heavily leans towards aesthetics, it finds, in Africa, an engagement peculiar to the African socio-political condition. In spite of its claim to high culture, poetry in Africa has not shied away from issues that concern the growth and development of the continent. Rather, poetry has been preoccupied with the question of humanity, of nationhood, of political regeneration, and of civil society.

With the cultural turn towards the end of the Twentieth century, poetry the world over has sought to unhinge itself from high culture in order to thematise issues that were in the modernist temper, seen only as fit for the sphere of popular or mass culture. It therefore, resists any confinement to the domain of mythology, individualism, or elevated aestheticism. Rather, it seeks to critique the spheres of human life, to interrogate humanity. One way poetry interrogates humanity is through its capacity to speak to power. While there are views that contest the stance of poetry as a critique of socio-political condition of society, African poetry in European languages, in diverse forms and to different degrees, continues to versify issues and realities that impact directly on the lives of the peoples of Africa. Our concern in this chapter is to demonstrate the engagement of emerging poetic voices in Africa with mainly political issues that have become rather perennial to the continent. Like many thinkers in Africa past and present these poets seem to see Africa's condition of underdevelopment mainly from the viewpoint of political failure. Their poetry thus, becomes heavily inflected with political tone. The chapter also provides insight into the dimension of exile in their poetry, which is linked to the question of leadership failure on the continent. The analytic method here is mainly sociological and contextual, although emphasis is also placed on artistic peculiarity. Poetry in this context is conceived as a cultural critique, in the same class of other artworks such as music, performance, story-telling and other cultural productions. These are used to challenge the powers of the establishment and question the complacency of civil society. From a close reading of selected texts, the fears and hopes of new African poets (poets whose works are relatively unknown) for their continent are highlighted. While the concerns raised in their poetry are not new – because their precursors have effectively thematised the same fears and hopes – a peculiar tenor of lamentation is discovered in their diverse tones. They appear more frustrated than their precursors. Like other thinkers they wonder aloud through their poetry why certain problems persist on th continent. Among many others, the poets include Remi Raji, Uche Nduka, Mildred Barya, Abigail George, Dzekashu MacViban, Fungisayi Sasa and Chiedu Ezeanah.

Literary Trajectory

There is a need to contextualise the terms 'the emerging poetic voices in Africa' or 'new African poets'. They imply poets that have appeared on the literary scene since the 1990s. This period is decades away from the beginning of African poetry in European languages which began during the colonial period, with poets such as Gabriel Okara, Dennis Osadebey, Nnamdi Azikiwe, Crispin George, Gladys Casely Hayford, and a number of others, whom Donatus I. Nwoga (1979:32–56) refers to as 'pioneer poets'. Okara, whose poems first appeared in *Black Orpheus* in 1957 (the other aforementioned poets had appeared in various forums before him), is often credited with starting what has come to be regarded as modern African poetry in English. For instance, Nwoga contends that 'Okara suddenly made public a new direction, a new intensity, a new vigour which did not exist in any poetry in English that preceded it' (1979:33). In the following years, more poets in European languages emerged, as colonial education conquered Africa. The poets studied in this chapter are, therefore, descendants of poets who are either dead or alive, no longer write or are still writing. Given the literary productions in Africa since the colonial time, the new poets emerged into a literary tradition that some see as dynamic – a tradition that by the mid-1980s had produced the first black African Nobel Laureate for literature, Wole Soyinka.

While the issue of periodisation – that is, the splitting of literary productions into generations in Africa – is questionable, and has in fact engendered a debate, it is useful for us to conceive of these younger poets as a generation, in the loose sense of the word.[1] One of the conceptual problems in this regard is to clearly differentiate the poetry of those we call new African poets from the poetry of those who have been on the scene since the beginning and are still writing, such as Okara. To do this requires, on the one hand, recourse to historicity, the epochs in the life of Africa that have profoundly inhered themselves on poetic discourse; on the other hand, it demands an analytic focus on both the individual and the collective aesthetic choices the poets have had to make with regards to the idioms that best serve their moments of poetic growth and maturity. Guided, as it were, by historicity and aesthetic choices, we may safely talk – as other critics have previously done – of the pre-independence nationalist era, the post-independence disillusionment era, and the era of despondency (beginning roughly in the 1990s), marked by an extreme form of angst, near total pessimism, and the urgency to emigrate from Africa.

The pre-independence nationalist era, what we would regard as the first generation of African poetry in European languages, concerns itself, as the term implies, with a high degree of nationalist imagination. Schooled in, and deeply influenced by, Euro-American modernism (which was the subject of attack in Chinweizu and 's Towards the De-colonisation of African Literature), the poets evolved, in their time, what should be better seen as a pastiche of idioms (both local and foreign) to articulate individual aspirations in the context of nations yearning for independence from colonial empires. Remarkable poets of this era such as Senghor, p'Bitek, Kofi Awoonor, Dennis Brutus, and others evoke a poetic discourse that is a fusion of private (artistic) yearnings and public cries for de-colonisation.

The roaring 1960s brought flag independence to Africa. But it was not to be celebrated, as Ayi Kwei Armah's *The Beautyful Ones Are Not Yet Born* alerts Africans. Instead of the happiness that should come with freedom, Africa was thrown into disillusionment. And poetic voices emerged, most loudly in Nigeria after the civil war (1967–70), to confront power and its permutations in high places. With Odia Ofeimun's *The Poet Lied* (notice the tone of insolence in the title), Niyi Osundare's *Songs of the Marketplace*, Kofi Anyidoho's *Elegy for the Revolution* (echoing Armah's title above), and Jack Mapanje's *Of Chameleon and Gods*, a new regime of protest poetry took centre stage, speaking directly to power, and insisting on the agency of poetry for social change, the performative dimension of the poetic discourse. The emergence of this generation coincided with the heyday of Marxism in Africa; indeed some of the poets, such as Osundare, regarded themselves as Marxists. Osundare, perhaps the most prolific of his generation, would insist on what he sees as the demystification and de-mythologising of African poetry; that is to say, poetry – following the argument of Chinweizu et al. – should emanate, as a matter of aesthetic expediency, from African traditional poetics, and should become not only meaningful to ordinary people but should also, in a Marxist spirit, champion their cause. From his much-quoted meta-poem, 'Poetry Is', to his polemical essays such as 'The Writer as Righter', Osundare has sought to map out a direction for the poetic discourse of his generation. In contesting the established notion of poetry as an arm of high culture, a mytho-individualistic aesthetic that uncompromisingly excludes the ordinary, less educated, people in the society, Osundare contends that:

> Poetry is
> the hawker's ditty
> the eloquence of the gong
> the lyric of the marketplace
> the luminous ray
> on the grass's morning dew. (Songs of the Marketplace, pp. 3–4)

Ordinary people, such as the hawker in Osundare's estimation, partake in the aesthetic process of poetry. The 'gong' is a metaphorical reference to the bucolic community in Africa where the (so-called) 'unlettered' make and enjoy eloquent poetry. The marketplace, considered too commonplace for the kind of poetry received from the West, is – if we listen carefully – filled with local lyricism which according to Osundare, is poetry itself. This conception of poetry seemed to appeal to most of the poets of the post-independence era. Beyond the revaluation of the poetics handed down to them, the poets also argue that poetry should be ideologically potent enough to speak on behalf of the oppressed masses.

The thesis put forward by the Osundare generation would impact greatly on the evolution of the new poets focussed on this work. The reason for this is not far-fetched. The Osundare generation, in clearing the space for itself, embarked on a theorisation of what it considered the right kind of poetry for Africa, a continent despoiled by its political leaders. They consequently presented a poetry that was bold and courageous in demanding social equality. The new poets would find this appealing because they were born into the socio-political condition that the poetry had historicised. The new poets also found appeal in the collective aesthetic choice of the Osundare generation, which rests on the notion that poetry ought to be rooted in indigenous orature. However, unlike the Osundare generation, the new poets are pessimistic in their vision – perhaps, as a result of the frustration that comes with a continent seemingly growing worse despite the artistic intervention from earlier poets and writers. It is this frustration that has caused the migration of some writers and intellectuals out of Africa. But in spite of their rhizomic tendency or the dispersal trope conspicuous in their poetry, the poets are concerned about the fate of their nations, about the plight of people in Africa, and continue to write poems that confront power with the awareness that Africa's problems remain largely political.

Nation, Power and Dissidence

While it may sound like an undue generalisation that African poetry, of whatever generation and artistic temperament, is essentially political and anti-establishment in nature, it is valid to assert that African poets, like writers of all genres, have seen themselves as operating in social conditions that they do not like. Even without intending to, their works often end up historicising this condition. But many of them have expressed their disenchantment with their nation's political situation, and have intended their works to relate their philosophical standpoints on such a situation with a view to stirring conscience and spurring actions against what they see as the ineptitude of the establishment. Indeed, in the last century, writers in Africa have suffered (in some cases, extreme) molestation from the rulers. Ngugi wa Thiong'o, who suffered a long incarceration because of his writing, notes in *Writers in Politics* that 'whether actively involved in political struggle or not, many African writers have often found that the very subject matter of their poems has placed them on the wrong side of the ruling cliques' (1985:69). Ngugi's kin in the writing profession, Micere Githae Mugo, puts it in a blunt way: 'most writers under neo-colonial dictatorships find their creativity censored, stifled, and targeted for vicious attack by the system. Through the use of terror, the offending systems go all out to impose silence in yet another effort to close another channel for raising the consciousness of the people' (1997:84). Mugo is here speaking from experience, having been condemned to imprisonment on account of her writing and theatre work.

The social vision of the African writer has, therefore, been located at the juncture where the desire, even urgency, of 'raising consciousness' or narrating nation clashes with the self-glorifying discourse of power in Africa; a discourse that presents even the worst despot in the garb of messianism. Michel Foucault in one of his deliberations on power states that '[the] most intense point of lives, the one where their energy is concentrated, is precisely there where they clash with power, struggle with it, endeavour to utilise its forces or to escape its traps' (1979:80).

For African writers, the decades of post-independence despotism in Africa, and the current condition of pseudo-democracies, have formed the 'intense point of lives' as they continue to clash with power in the form of protest poetry. In the past decades, it was even imperative for some African poets and writers (Okigbo, Soyinka, Brutus) to go out on the streets in demonstrations, or engage in other courageous activities, in addition to writing subversive poetry because the despotic regimes themselves had the double strategy of physically assaulting the people, as reported in the media, and of using the mass media (radio, television, newspaper) to perpetrate anti-human activities and to perpetuate themselves in power. But it is the cultural form of counter-discourse that the poets have most effectively deployed. Sara Mills points out that '[p]articularly through their verbal dexterity and use of language, those who are not in economically powerful positions may nevertheless manage to negotiate for themselves fairly powerful positions in the hierarchy' (1997:40). Through their powerful threnodic tones, or insistent tenor of counter-discourse, African poets vividly dramatise a capacity to engage power in ideological combat.

Across the generations, we see this ideological combat, in disparate idioms, in diverse tones. For instance, in the subdued, almost unrealised love between the personas in Arthur Nortje's poetry (1971), there is the angst invested in lines such as 'we have long survived the stigma of being' ('Continuation' 28–9); there is a powerful orchestration of 'aches' underneath what one might see as Nortje's visceral optimism in historicising apartheid. When Jared Angira (1972), in the intense, insistent voice he raises on behalf of 'silent voices', declares that 'the torch / shall burn / your mutilated conscience / and wake up / from the powdered chamber' ('Epilogue' 19), it is clear that he is here in his usual combat with power.

Following their precursors, emerging African poets whose voices are growing sturdier in the twenty-first century choose to combat power, realising their aesthetic of resistance by addressing social issues in their immediate societies. These issues encapsulate individual experiences that the poet perceives in the larger context of the society. For instance, the Nigerian poet, Nnimmo Bassey (1998), imprisoned during the dictatorship of the late General Sani Abacha, composes this poem which foregrounds the inevitability of hoping in the face of tyranny:

> Don't tell me now how it
> Feels
> To see your liberty bowed by boots
> Don't tell me now how it
> Tastes
> To have vinegar down your throat
> Don't tell me what you'll do
> For when we are out then we'll growl
> Don't ask me when we'll be
> Out
> For if we knew then we won't
> Don't ask me why we
> Hope
> Is the only sure thing they cannot jail. ('Intercepted', p. 11)

The condition of prison, thus, does not baulk at the invention or re-invention of hope. The 'boots', with the capacity to suppress people's 'liberty', is a synecdochic reference to the military junta and the reign of despotism in Africa under which people's freedoms are stifled. The image we have here of military power is one that cannot be surpassed; the caged personas (notice the 'we' in the poem) cannot by any action extricate themselves. But one thing they can continue to do, in the view of this poet, is to hope. The poem itself is symbolic of the age in which this generation of poets live: an age in which, given all the past political failures (and the failure of counter-discourse to arrest the failures), the new poets see their societies as huge prisons where the very act of writing is to hope.

Apart from speaking to power through personal experiences, as Bassey does above, there is also the strategy of dramatising, through vivid description, the state of struggle, the level of hardship and despair, in the society. Through such dramatisation, the poet indicts the establishment and interrogates the complacency of the elite. The poet, in this case, shows the realities of existence and implicitly reviles the political leaders for causing the harsh realities. The young South African poet, Abigail George (2011) in her poem 'Orange Farm on the 7 O'clock News' paints the picture of a collapsed system where mayhem holds sway. The first stanza of the poem shows a clash between people's will and power:

> Machine guns go da-da-da-da-da-da-da-da-da-da-da-da-da
> Drowning out the swaying, barefoot crowds in the streets
> Shooting rubber bullets through the air although they aren't aimed to kill
> Beating down half-defeated men and women, civilians on foot.
> Absent parents: children out of sight, out of mind. (lines 1–5)

The staccato machine guns are symbolic of the existing power and, as the following lines show, are stalling the force of the people's will. Whether it is rubber or live bullets (the poem is ironic here in the light of the so-called 'rubber bullets' drowning out the people from the streets), the picture we have is of a group of demonstrators being overcome by the superior power of the gun, even though they are resilient as indicated in the metaphor 'barefoot'. Their resilience is seen all through. At Orange Farm, where the crisis is set, the people have resolved to confront the establishment: 'everyone is up in arms about this' (line 13). This is in spite of the hunger, of living in 'dirty slums'. The poet places this in the larger context of a continent in retrogression:

> The beautiful dream: the rainbow, the African renaissance
> Counting every two steps forward we take three back
> We move forward and backward like a river seemingly with ease
> What about the orphans who seek shelter from the rules of the wild
> Children who play in time with toy handguns and grenades, toy soldiers. (lines 21–5)

The poet evokes the theme of child soldier, a ubiquitous phenomenon across Africa in the last decades and symptomatic of a degenerate existence. What the poet actually implies here is that Africa, by abandoning its orphans to 'the rules of the wild', has killed its future; without children there is no prospect for the continent.

The description can also be that of a lack of technological necessity that is peculiar to the poet's immediate society, as we see in Chiedu Ezeanah's 'The Blackout' (2011). The images in the poem are quite striking:

> Swooped by a blackout
> another day outages
> into the stone-age
> seeking a spark.
>
> The noxious relief of plants
> in the hub of darkness
> tinders homes and breaths.
>
> The sky's solar eye dimmed
> by infernal flares yields
> the monochrome of night.
> Knees still bleed, suppliant,
> unsung in the extinguishing light.
>
> Our only Republic beams darkness –
> where does the light live, and bless?

For years, Nigeria has faced the problem of electricity. The problem is seen here from a poet's eye. In the poet's view, the constant power outages give the society the aura of the Stone Age. That is to say, the nation is moving backward instead of forward. But also the dominant image of darkness directs our attention to the inability of this 'Republic' to have any positive developmental vision. The metaphor 'Republic' is better seen as the power that controls the political decisions of the society; and it is, as the poem implies, indicted for the condition of darkness in which the people live. As the poem intimates, it is not only humans who are adversely affected by the erratic power supply in the society, but also non-humans such as plants, houses and the sky.

The critique also comes in the form of the poet-persona addressing her nation, as we see in Fungisayi Sasa's ironically titled poem 'Anthem' (2011). The poet invents her own song of allegiance for her nation, but it is laden with her deep frustration with the nation's stagnancy. She knows why the nation is in that state, and that is why she feels sad; the nation is being brutalised by those who claim to be its leaders:

> You are beautiful, my Zimbabwe,
> though the sharp words of corrupt men
> are the heavy, hard instruments
> raping you again; again and again,
> though the stench of a government's
> betrayal is raw sewage fermenting in your streets
> and even though your children lick the pus
> from their wounds so that hunger may be appeased.
> You are still beautiful. (lines 1–10)

The poet's nationalism is embedded in the line 'You are beautiful'. It is not a mere compliment, but an expression of an abiding bond between the poet and her nation – a bond that spurs her to embark on a discourse that challenges power. The poet does not mince words in naming those she thinks have messed up the otherwise beautiful country. They are the 'corrupt men' who are part of the 'government's betrayal' that cause the raping of the nation. Notice the repetition of the word 'again' to emphasise the unending act of raping Zimbabwe has suffered from. And when the home country is repeatedly raped, it is the citizenry, especially those who are economically weak and politically voiceless, who suffer most. The poet refers to those as 'children' who 'lick the pus / from their wounds'. This is a strong image that evokes helplessness, because a people, in order to feed, would resort to licking the pus of their own wounds; that is, eating the wastes that come out of their own bodies. This conveys the intensity of the hardship the people are thrown into because of the raping of the nation by the political elite. But the poet is hopeful that the nation and its citizenry may be free some day:

> Tsvarakadenga, stop your weeping
> and wash your face
> Discard your rags and oil your flesh
> Dance to summon the rains,
> chant to your ancestors who look at you now
> through hollow eyes.
> Abase yourself before the altar
> of a stone god with a clenched fist
> where your supplications cannot be heard. (lines 22–30)

Hope resonates, although the poem projects hope in a rather simplistic way. For a nation perpetually raped, for a citizenry condemned to licking the pus of their wounds (to maintain the poet's metaphor), what is required for emancipation ought to be a strong revolutionary movement, instead of merely hoping or soothing oneself with rhetoric of a better tomorrow or, as the last lines of the poem shows, surrendering oneself on the altar' of a god/goddess. But it is understandable, as the poem seems to imply that a people must be courageous enough to withstand any kind of conditions in which they find themselves. The ultimate goal of this poem is the foregrounding of a nation despoiled by its political elite, as we have seen in the previous poems. Power in such a context is in the hands of a few wicked, corrupt, and mindless persons who, contrary to what the people see in them, pose as great leaders and thinkers – even as messiahs – in a society that, as one of the poets has pointed out, grows backward.

Exile and Dispersal: Post-Nation Anxiety

There is a kind of cynicism that the new poets, like their precursors, might have undertaken an exercise in futility. This cynicism manifests itself in two ways.

Firstly, there are those who think the poets have invested so much utility in their art, regarding it as a means of struggle against a repressive authority; an authority mainly constituted by the political elite who, we may conjecture, rarely read poetry, or if they did, would hardly be disturbed by the force of the poem. This view is well expressed by the Nigerian scholar Wole Ogundele (2008) in an essay entitled 'An Appraisal of the Critical Legacies of the 1980s Revolution in Nigerian Poetry in English'. Juxtaposing the poetics of the Okigbo–Soyinka generation (the pre-independence nationalist period) and that of the Osundare generation (the period of post-independence disillusionment), Ogundele wonders what the overtly instrumentalist ideology of the post-independence period has achieved. If the poets, in their Marxist aesthetics, have set out to confront the cruel leadership of their nations, then to what extent has that aim been achieved? In Ogundele's view, 'if the politicians learnt no lessons from the poetry of the [pre-independence nationalist] period because it was "too obscure", they learnt none either from the prose and drama of the [post-independence disillusionment] era which surely, were both "more accessible" and more "political and socially relevant"' (2008:144). It is Ogundele's contention (as it is the contention of many other scholars) that the Alter-Native ideology (trumpeted by the post-independence poets) – the ideology inherent in the present generation – is counterproductive.

Secondly, there are those (including Ogundele) who think that the poets, by focusing too much on what they perceive as their social engagement, mortgage the craft of poetry for its purported interventionist role. The British scholar, Stewart Brown (2003), is one such thinker. Brown opines that '[while] there can be no doubting these [new] poets' sincerity or the depth of their anguish, the unending self-righteousness of the narrative voice, the artless predictability of the sentiments and the clichéd language of "protest" undermine…the force of so many of these poems, *as poems*' ('Still Daring the Beast', 101). Such critical (indeed cynical) positions have been met with counter-arguments. In the preface to his volume, *A Song from Exile*, Olu Oguibe (1990), one of the earliest voices of new generation, writes,

> It is arguable to what extent the artist can influence or turn the course of history, and we in Nigeria have had so long a historyof battles between the artist and the state that we have even greater reason to be doubtful…. [But] we are simply saying what we see, for it is seeing and not saying, our people say, that kills the elder.
>
> It is hearing and not heeding that will kill the child. That, for us, is the fate of the emperor and the poet. (1990:7)

This is just one strand of the defence, with other poets such as Remi Raji (see his preface to *A Harvest of Laughters*) claiming that they are moved to soothe the pain of the suffering masses.

The foregoing scenario is remarkable in the sense that it is on the one hand symptomatic of the debate surrounding the entire foundation of African literature in European languages, which is often charged with being heavily anthropological and sociological, of being too thematically-concentrated, and of being self-limiting. For instance, Charles E. Nnolim in an essay entitled 'African Literature in the Twenty-first Century: Challenges for Writers and Critics' argues that African writers, instead of perpetually binding themselves to Africa's unending socio-political problems, should concentrate on 'forward-looking' literature that imagines a 'utopia for Africa' (2006:6). He wonders why Africans do not write science fiction or do not write much about peoples of other nations and continents.[2] On the other hand, the scenario arguably informs the phenomenon of exile or the central trope of dispersal dominant in the new generation of African poetry in English. In the late 1980s and the first half of the 1990s, almost all of the new poets were living in Africa, some of them having just earned their first or second degrees. But now, several of them, especially from Nigeria, have moved to the Western world. In the words of Toyin Adewale, herself a poet of this generation, the new Nigerian poets 'chose to go into voluntary exile' (2000: iii) during the dictatorship of the late General Sani Abacha.

But the new Nigerian poets – and their counterparts in other nations of Africa – could conveniently already be prisoners and exiles in their own country. Indeed, their migration out of Nigeria is merely a second level of exile. Exile here is conceived broadly as what David Bevan calls 'a constant of our common predicament' in which case it is 'a form of estrangement [...and] otherness'. Exile, in its intensity, is thus synonymous with prison condition. The notion of exile as a condition of prison is the main focus of the book *The Word behind Bars and the Paradox of Exile* edited by the Ghanaian poet and scholar, Kofi Anyidoho (1977). In his introduction 'Prison as Exile/Exile as Prison: Circumstances, Metaphor, and a Paradox of Modern African Literatures', Anyidoho emphasises the perennial leadership crisis in Africa which has, through various indices, reduced the continent to a huge prison in which its writers see themselves as exiles. 'The focus on exile and prison', Anyidoho writes, 'as two sides of the experience of oppression was almost inevitable, considering that intellectuals and creative artists who insist on fighting oppression often end up in prison, that those who manage to survive prison often end up in exile' (1977:3). Most new African poets (including the older ones) who emigrated to the West during dictatorships in Africa would claim that if they had not left the continent, they would have been killed. Such claims could not be far from the truth given the fact that the Nigerian ruler, Sani Abacha, at one point declared Wole Soyinka wanted for treasonable offence; worse still was the judicial murder of Ken Saro-Wiwa in 1995 by the Abacha regime.

Exile, whether in the form of estrangement within one's society or emigration to another country, affects the poetry of the new African poets thematically and stylistically. The trope of dispersal comes to dominate the poems they write in exile. This trope exhibits a vivid awareness of *being* (thematically, stylistically) among other peoples, literatures, cultures, styles, voices and so on. The form is ultimately characterised by pastiche; and the content by a social text that explores, in diverse ways, the triumphs and travails of multiculturalism and postmodernism. The postmodern practice among these new African poets is particularly obvious in the way some of the poets, having settled outside the continent, now tend to distance themselves from the literary tradition from which they emerged. In the larger context of some African scholars' hostility to postmodernism and post-structuralism, their poetry expectedly encounters criticisms such as that of Niyi Osundare where he refers to the poets as the CNN generation.[2] For some scholars and observers, these poets are straying away from what might be considered their original literary tradition or the *authentic* tradition of African writing. They are lured by the competing cultures of what Fredric Jameson (1998) insists is late capitalism or what has come to be strangely regarded by others as 'glocalisation'

But the other side of the argument is expressed by Abiola Irele (1990). There is no period of Nigerian or African writing, in Irele's view, that does not have a 'historical and thematic correspondence' to that of European, American, or world literatures. In this premise, the postmodern practice of the new African poets (dispersal, pastiche, multiculturalism) is one such correspondence whereby the poets who exile themselves in Europe and America succumb to the pressures and influences of glocalisation.

This entire phenomenon is referred to here as post-nation anxiety. Unlike the poems discussed before, the poems written in exile or subjected to the trope of exile and dispersal critique cultural issues beyond the anxiety of nationhood, although the issues they raise are indirectly connected with the question of power on the continent. In the poem simply titled 'Exodus' by the Cameroonian Dzekashu MacViban (2011), there is another form of angst; a deep sense of frustration, not with the power of the political elite of an African nation, but with the instability and the unsettled life of exile.

> Out went we, with flocks and herds
> Out of Pharaoh's custody, seeking
> The Promised Land. Songs of deliverance
> Rose from griots and gongs – tore
> Tore the air with liberation-lyrics.
> Our marriage – now a vague dream –
> Was some distant lore of how
> WE LIVED IN DEATH. (lines 1–8)

'Pharaoh' in this poem is a figurative representation of the kind of power the poets confront in Africa. The persona has moved out of the Pharaoh's nation ('Pharaoh's custody'), and assumes that the 'Promised Land' – an obvious reference to the developed world – will turn out to be a place where she can dream and achieve her dream. If the home country were good, governed not by Pharaoh but by Moses, there would be no need to go into exile. But exile turns out to be what the poet calls 'the wilderness of Sinai' – the full import of this metaphor can better be accessed through the biblical story of the children of Israel spending over forty years to reach the Promised Land which is otherwise not far from Egypt. The poet here is of course drawing our attention to the disturbing gap between the dream of achieving success in the Promised Land, the land of exile, and the lack of achieving such success due to the vagaries of living in exile. Most young Africans, including the self-exiled writers, think once they are out of Africa they can fully realise their dreams, but it usually does not turn out to be so. The life of the exile comes to be characterised by distress and disenchantment, as the lines here show: 'We moved under the watchful eyes of the sun / As mirages danced at a distance / Could it be our promised land? Our hearts beat' (16–18). The heartbeat here is that of confusion. Between living in exile and returning to dysfunctional society in Africa, the persona keeps asking: could the West be his promised land?

The Nigerian poet Uche Nduka would be considered by many as one of the emerging poets in Africa who has, more than his contemporaries, versified the condition of exile. He moved to Germany in the 1990s, having published *Flower Child* and *The Second Act* in Nigeria. The first poetry volume he published outside Nigeria is suggestively titled *The Bremen Poems*. It exhibits an obvious shift in Nduka's thematic concern and stylistic inclination (see Oha 2005:1–19). The poems become shorter, the lines shorter; and the metaphors, growing purer, organise themselves with sparks of intensity. Since *The Bremen Poems*, Nduka's poems have assumed a curious level of brevity, weighty with paradoxes, and oxymoronic witticisms. They grow further away from referential exigencies, foregrounding their images and sonic essences rather than directing readers' attention to any semantic mapping. Although latent in *Flower Child and Second Act*, it is in *The Bremen Poems*, and subsequent volumes, that Nduka turns his attention to erotic themes, very individualistic, which are capable of revealing the personal odyssey of an artist. The first poem in *The Bremen Poems* betrays this shift in thematic focus:

> Even in so divine a time
> she screams and dreams
> She walks on the freeway
> where everyone walks
> Everywhere in the ballroom
> of the mind you find her
> But where nights void her legtraps, no man comes.

This, even for the persona, sounds strange and it reveals the freedom and its concomitant loneliness in a society so different. This is in sharp contrast to the society, where a woman cannot dream, cannot even scream, and is not free to walk, where 'everyone walks'; and for a woman to be found in a 'ballroom' of the mind amounts to immorality. The case is different here, and in this collection, Nduka crafts poems to dramatise this primal disparity. For instance, in the poem 'To Your Cigarette', Nduka demonstrates that the European woman with her cigarette seems to wall herself against the worries of the world. He says of her: 'no pain bloodies your lips' (p. 3), a phenomenon that is common in his own society. While one agrees with readings such as Oha's that poets' attachments to places are often expressed through erotic images; and that for Nduka, 'imagining the space as female becomes particularly a revelation of the desire to possess and be possessed by the exile space' (p. 8), it is more useful to see the referent of Nduka's body of amorous images not as the physical place or space of exile (so that the love is imagined as existing between the poet and the city), but as a collective of experiences which the poet has had with different individuals. For Nduka, experience has no boundary. His erotic images such as we encounter in the volume *Heart's Field* (with a photo of a naked Nduka as front cover), undermine the claim that his love trope stops at the level of his attachment to a city or exile space.

Beyond the open surprise at the different life that the poet now has to live, there is a deep sense of nostalgia articulated in such poems as 'I Speak of River', 'Note to a Season', 'Far from this Sadness', and others in *The Bremen Poems*. In 'Like the Dark Sky', we encounter this nostalgia:

> Like the dark sky
> hungering for stars,
> my lips long for
> the flute of wine's fire;
> for a sun
> to disrobe desire on the wire.

This nostalgic longing has become a strong theme running through Nduka's poetry volumes written in exile. It shows the poet-persona misses his homeland, and would have gladly stayed in his nation, if it had not been messed up by its political elite. This could be said of most of the poems written in exile by emerging African voices. They have left home, vacated the nationalist theme, and now have to contend with the theme of survival in exile. Their frustration about life in exile is also a frustration about life on the continent, which up till now has failed to improve.

Conclusion

The concept of poetry as cultural critique rests on the notion that poetry as an art does not limit itself to mere artistic orchestrations; it seeks to find as its substance socio-political issues that concern humanity. In this regards, the poet feels compelled to use the poetic medium to participate in any kind of discourse that has an impact on the life of the society. It has been our contention in this chapter that the emerging voices in African poetry have, like their precursors, used poetry to critique the pressing socio-political issues on the continent. Because the poets – indeed many thinkers in Africa – predicate the issues on the question of poor leadership and the near absence of good governance, their poetic discourse is largely antithetical to the establishment of political power in Africa. In their estimation, Africa has failed to develop because of the kind of leadership it has had.

By writing poetry, these poets hope that they are not only exposing the realities that negate the self-glorifying rhetoric of the political elite in Africa, but are also helping to dethrone the power of such political elites. But it does seem that power is not easily dethroned. This informs the exodus of these poets, writers and other intellectuals out of Africa. Life in exile presents other existential problems. The object of critique, for the new poetry, thus shifts from the concern with the nation to a post-nation anxiety which entails the historicising of survival struggles in exile. Any critique of the condition of exile points indirectly to the power behind the retrogression in Africa. This is the assumption that if Africa had been well-governed and developed, there would have been no need for the exilic condition dramatised in the poetry.

Notes

1. For opposing views on the debate, see Garuba (2005:51–72) and Obiwu (2006: 37–43).
2. See for instance Part XI of the seminal book *African Literature: An Anthology of Criticism and Theory* edited by Tejumola Olaniyan and Ato Quayson (2007) for the debate on post-structuralism and postmodernism from the perspective of African literature. Also see the chapter 'African Literature and the Crisis of Post-Structuralist Theorising' in Niyi Osundare's (2002) *Thread in the Loom: Essays on African Literature and Culture.*

References

Adewale, Toyin, 2000, 'Introduction', in *25 New Nigerian Poets*, Berkeley: Ishmael Reed Publishing.

Angira, Jared, 1972, *Silent Voices*, London: Heinemann.

Anyidoho, Kofi, 1977, 'Prison as Exile/Exile as Prison: Circumstances, Metaphor, and a Paradox of Modern African Literature', in Kofi Anyidoho, ed., *The Word Behind the Bars and the Paradox of Exile*, Illinois: Northwestern University Press.

Bassey, Nnimmo, 1998, *Intercepted*, Ibadan: Kraft Books.

Brown, Stewart, 2003, 'Still Daring the Beast: Niyi Osundare and Contemporary *Nigerian Poetry*', in Abdul-Rasheed Na'Allah, ed., *The People's Poet: Emerging Perspectives on Niyi Osundare*, Trenton, NJ: Africa World Press.

Ezeanah, Chiedu, 2011, 'The Blackout', 15 August, <http://www.AfricanWriter.com/articles/513/1/Angst-Flaring---Poems-by-Chiedu-Ezeanah/Page1.html>

Foucault, Michel, 1979, 'The Life of Infamous Men', in eds, Meaghan Morris and Paul Patton, *Michel Foucault: Power, Truth, Strategy*, Sydney: Feral Publications.

Garuba, Harry, 2005, 'The Unbearable Lightness of Being: Re-figuring Trends in Recent Nigerian Poetry', *English in Africa* 32 (1):51–72.

George, Abigail, 2011, 'Orange Farm on the 7 O'clock News', 15 August, <http://www.AfricanWriter.com/articles/542/1/Reading-the-Bones---Poems-by-Abigail-George/Page1.html>

Irele, Abiola, 1990, *The African Experience in Literature and Ideology*, Bloomington and Indianapolis: Indiana University Press.

Jameson, Fredric, 1998, *The Cultural Turn: Selected Writings on the Postmodern 1983–1998*, London: Verso.

MacViban, Dzekashu, 2011, 'Exodus, 6 September, <http://thenewblackmagazine.com/view.aspx?index=2680>

Mills, Sara, 1997, *Discourse*. London & New York: Routledge.

Mugo, Micere Githae, 1997, 'Exile and Creativity: A Prolonged Writer's Block' Kofi Anyidoho, ed., *The Word Behind the Bar and the Paradox of Exile*, Illinois Northwestern University Press.

Nnolim, Charles, 2006, 'African Literature in the twenty-first Century: Challenges for Writers and Critics', *African Literature Today. 25*, Ibadan: Heinemann.

Nortje, Arthur, 1971, *Dead Roots*, London: Heinemann.

Nwoga, Donatus, 1979, 'Modern African Poetry: the Domestication of a Tradition', Eldred Durosimi Jones, ed., *African Literature Today. 10.*
Obiwu, O., 2006, 'The History of Nigerian Literature, 1772–2006', *Farafina* (7):37–43.
Oha, Obododimma, 2005, 'En/countering the New Language of Exile in Uche Nduka's *The Bremen Poems*', *Portal Journal of Multidisciplinary International Studies* 2 (1): 1–19.
Oguibe, Olu, 1990, *A Song from Exile*, Bayreuth: Boomerang Press.
Ogundele, Wole, 2008, 'An Appraisal of the Critical Legacies of the 1980s Revolutionin Nigerian Poetry in English', Aderemi Raji-Oyelade and Oyeniyi Okunoye, eds, *The Postcolonial Lamp: Essays in Honour of Dan Izevbaye*, Ibadan: Bookcraft.
Olaniyan, Tejumola and Ato Quayson, 2007, *African Literature: An Anthology of Criticism and Theory*, Malden, MA and Oxford: Wiley Blackwell.
Osundare, Niyi, 1983, *Songs of the Marketplace*, Ibadan: New Horn Press.
Osundare, Niyi, 2002, *Thread in the Loom: essays on African literature and culture,* Trenton, NJ: Africa World Press.
Sasa, Fungisayi, 2011, 'Anthem', 6 September, <http://www.AfricanWriter.com/articles/434/1/Myths-and-Legends---Poems-by-Fungisayi-Sasa/Page1.html>
wa Thiong'o, Ngugi, 1997, *Writers in Politics: A Re-Engagement with Issues of Literature and Society*, Oxford: James Currey.

5

African Literature and the Anxiety of Being in the Twenty-first Century

Stephen Ogundipe

Introduction

Much attention has been paid to the legacies of African literature in the Twentieth century articulating the overarching social-economic, political and cultural rupture on the continent. Unique moments in the historical trajectory of African literature and the distinctive marks made by generations of African writers have also been captured in various critical works. The general opinion is that the first two generations of African writers have responded positively in terms of recovering Africa's lost humanity and projecting African personality in their writings. But there remains the need to articulate how contemporary African literature has expressed the fears and challenges of living in Africa in the twenty-first century.

This chapter highlights the contributions of the new generation of African writers to developmental issues. While acknowledging conflicting critical standpoints on the contributions of new literary works, the essay suggests that critical issues relating to identity, language and social vision of African literature should be addressed. This brings up the practical application of the electronic media, the internet and related technological platforms as new paradigms of knowledge for African literary engagement.

African literature has experienced tremendous growth and gained notable recognition through the works of many African writers since the middle of the Twentieth century. This recognition is attested by the annual Nobel Prize for literature already won by four distinguished African writers: Wole Soyinka (Nigerian, 1986) Naguib Mahfouz (Egyptian, 1993), Nadine Gordimer (South African, 2003) and J. M. Coetzee (South African, 2006). African writers have also won other prestigious international laurels such as the Booker Prize and the Caine Prize for African Writing. The incredible amount of literary output, the variety of literary forms and the quality of aesthetics of works by African writers have also enhanced the ratings of African literature on the international literary scene.

Conceptualising African Literature

'African literature' is not as easy to define as it might first appear. It is such a vast and diverse phenomenon that can hardly be captured in a simple attempt at definition. The term is frequently used to refer to literature written about Africa in European languages. But it entails far more than this. Such a narrow perspective fails to give consideration to the substantial indigenous literary traditions in Africa, and the literatures associated with Arabic speaking areas of Africa. It is worth observing that African literature is often limited to south of Sahara, leaving out North Africa. Tejumola Olaniyan and Ato Quayson (2007:6) sum up this conceptual problem when they assert that African literature 'has suffered from either too much or too little acknowledgement of its many contexts'. The question of the validity and identity of African literature remains unresolved after several decades.

Since the Makerere, Dakar and Freetown conferences on African literature, held between 1962 and 1963, scholars have persistently raised the question of whether African literature is an entity in itself or an extension of European literature. Critical evaluations have often drawn attention to the problematic of the language of expression, notably those of Ngugi wa Thiong'o (1986), Abiola Irele (1990), Anthony Appiah (1992), Daniel Kunene (1992), and Shina Afolayan (2002). The arguments of these scholars recognize the ambiguous relationship of African literature with European culture, and the contradictions of the historical situation of colonialism. The nature of African literature, the medium of its production and of its discussion have continued to pose problems to commentators over the decades.

The critical issue of language in African literature engaged early on the attention of Obi Wali in his famous essay 'The Dead End of African Literature'. According to Wali, 'until African literature is written in African languages, African writers would be merely pursuing a dead end (1963:14). This suggests that the uncritical acceptance of the language of the colonialists (English, French and Portuguese) as the medium of writing has no chance of advancing African literature. However this position is limited by its over-generalization. Half a century after this statement was made, there is no doubt that African writers have adapted the language of colonialists to serve African sensibilities.

Cheikh Anta Diop shared Obi Wali's perspective and sensibility when he argued that 'all literary works belong to the same language in which it i written' (1978:58). This is a misconception. Where, for instance, is 'the African language' that will promote 'African literature'? The obvious reality is that Africa is not a country, but a continent with hundreds of languages and cultures. This heterogeneity probably informs the position of writers such as Léopold Sédar Senghor, Ezekiel Mphalele and Chinua Achebe who regard European languages as a unifying force within African nations.

The privileging of English and other colonial languages is, however, not unslippery. For instance, this strategy fails to consider the multiplicity of traditions in African literature. Bernth Lindfors in 'A Last Shot at the 20th Century Canon', projects the kind of outlook that shows partiality for anglophone literature (2006). His list of thirty-six notable African writers, whose works have persistently attracted publishers' interest from 1976 to 1999, contains mostly anglophone writers. The writers on the list include Ayi Kwei Armah, Wole Soyinka, Buchi Emecheta, Bessie Head, Alex La Guma, Chinua Achebe, Cyprian Ekwensi, Dennis Brutus, Flora Nwapa, Nurudeen Farah, Ngugi wa Thiong'o, Ama Ata Aidoo, Amos Tutuola, Okot p'Bitek, Niyi Osundare, Femi Osofisan, Ben Okri, Tsitsi Danganrembga, Dambuso Marechera and Plaatje Ngema. According to Lindfors, these writers captured the unique and collective experiences of Africans before, during and after the colonial experience through their innovative and fascinating accounts.

No single tradition informs African literature. Given the multiple dimensions of the African literary tradition, it is imperative for scholars to be aware of the literary developments across African geographical and cultural boundaries. Keith Booker (1998), in a survey of the African novel, demonstrates this awareness in accounting for the different cultural, historical and political contexts of African literature. A survey of francophone African literature would be incomplete without highlighting the contributions of writers such as Ahmadou Kourouma, Hammidou Kane, Boubacar Diop, David Diop, Camara Laye, Aimé Césaire, Léopold Sénghor, Sembène Ousmane, Yambo Oulouguem, Mongo Beti, Aminata Sow Fall, Mariama Ba, David Diop, Ousmane Soce Diop, Ferdinand Oyono, Nafssatou Diallo, Calixthe Beyala, Sony Labou Tansi, Ken Bugul, Véronique Tadjo and a host of others.

Some of the important writers in Portuguese language within the context of African literature include Fernando Soromenho, Ruei de Noronha, Joao Dias and pathfinders such as Agostinho Neto, Aires de Almeida Santos, Jose Luandino Vieira, Baltasar Lepes, Jorgw Barbosa, Uanhenga Xitu, Jofre Rocha, Jose Graveirerinha, Noenina de Sousa, Malangatana, Ngwenya, Orlando Mendes, Antonio Quaclos, Naomia de Sousa, and Antonio Jacinto, who have contributed significantly to the representation of people's experience in lusophone Africa. North Africa has its own share of writers who elect to write in either French or Arabic. For example, Alifa Raifat, Nawal el-Sadawi, Naguib Mahfouz, Abdelhamid Benhedouga,

Hama Tuma, Tayeb Salih, Ezzedine Madani, Muhammad Dib, Kateb Yacine, Rachid Boudjedra, and Dris Chraibi among others.

Works of all the aforementioned authors from different parts of Africa provide a broader canvass through which one can encounter African literature with its multiplicity of subjects and divergence of literary and artistic styles.

African Literature in the Twenty-first Century

In spite of the appreciable recognition of African literature in the global context in the Twentieth century, the question remains how prepared is African literature for confronting the challenges of globalisation in the twenty-first century? What opportunities are available to African literature to re-position itself in the world? Can African literature advance socio-economic and political development in Africa in the Twenty-first century? These are questions that this article seeks to answer.

Much attention has been paid to reflections on the legacies of African literature in the Twentieth century. This is exemplified in critical studies such as Gbemisola Adeoti and Mabel Evwierhoma (2006) *After the Nobel Prize: Reflections on African Literature, Governance, and Development,* a special issue of Canadian Review of Comparative Literature entitled 'The Short Century and After: African Literatures and Cultures from 1945 to 2005', a special number of *Research in African Literatures*, and special editions of *African Literature Today* (ALT) with themes such as 'New Trends and Generations in African Literature' ALT 20, 'Childhood in African Literature' ALT 21, 'New Women Writing in African Literature' ALT 24, and 'New Directions in African Literature' ALT 25. All these publications capture unique moments in the historical trajectory of African literature, the vision, and the distinctive marks that have been made by generations of African writers. The consensus running through the publications is that the first two generations of African writers have responded positively in terms of recapturing Africa's lost humanity and projecting African personality in their writings.

In spite of the enviable achievement of the first two generations of African writers, certain scholars, however, take exceptions to the very 'narrow canvass' of African literature. Charles Nnolim (2006:1), for example, criticises the 'recurrent lamentations' of the past, present and future social political predicaments in the writings of the first two generations, calling for a change of focus.

But while some members of the new generation of African writers have addressed the same issues of governance and cultural dislocation that concerned their predecessors, others have focused in different directions from those of the early writers. The need to properly assess the contributions of the new generation of African writers has attracted two critical responses. Paul Zeleza (2007:9), for instance, describes the new generation as 'having more cosmopolitan visions of the African condition, cultural production, and the subjectivities of gender, class and sexuality'. A practical way of gauging this trend is exemplified in the short story collection, *To See the Mountain and other stories*, which consists of eighteen short stories, written by contributors from different parts of the continent. The manner in which some of the stories articulate the new realities and vibrancy of the new generation writing is illustrated below.

Noviolet Bulawayo's 'Hitting Budapest' is about a gang of six poverty stricken 'street children', who regularly visit a rich neighbourhood to harvest guavas as food. The parents in this story are represented as being irresponsible. While the children scavenge, 'mothers are busy with hair and talk, the fathers are playing draft'. A grandfather even impregnates his grand-daughter. The children, for their own part, have lost every sense of decency and innocence, as they despoil a suicide victim of her shoes in order to trade it for a loaf of bread. This is a departure from the traditional notion of the family as a caring and sustaining fulcrum.

Tim Keegan in 'What Molley knew' captures the circumstances surrounding the killing of a woman by her step-father. The mother of the victim fails to betray any emotion, when she learns of her daughter's murder. The story gives a distorted view of African motherhood, as her seeming stoicism suggests a rupture of filial bonding. This becomes more obvious when she discovers that her husband actually killed her daughter as a cover up for years of sexual abuse.

Lauri Kusurtsile's 'In the spirit of Mcphineas Lata' broaches the problem of sexual dissatisfaction in marriage. The failure of many husbands to satisfy their women sexually informs their resort to self-help by engaging a village lothario. The untimely death of the lothario, however, prompts the men to figure out what means can be employed to reclaim their women. This is achieved through information sharing by the men on the best strategies to satisfy their individual wives' sexual needs.

Beatrice Lamwaka's 'Butterfly dreams' addresses the menace of child soldiers in Africa. The conscription of children as soldiers in sectarian clashes in Africa ruptures the future of these young ones. The skinny outlook, bullet scars on once beautiful faces, cracked and swollen feet are physical manifestations of a greater psychological trauma, which child soldiers carry through life after demobilization. This is a very topical international issue which holds disturbing implications for the future of the continent. Judging from these stories, it is clear that the younger African writers are addressing different challenges facing the continent in different narrative modes. Like their predecessors they are conscious of their socio-political and economic realities, marking a kind of continuity and change in the nature of African literature.

The other concern of the new generation of African writers is registered in their explicitness, which has attracted some uncomplimentary criticism. Titi Adepitan

(2006:125), for instance, accuses some of the new writers of 'mixing literary tawdriness with more serious business'. In the opinion of Femi Osofisan (2009:31), 'the old notions of privacy, the consensual secretiveness and "holiness" that used to be attached to such matters as love and sex have long been axed and discarded as antiquated relic', by the new generation of writers. The sacrifice of bashfulness, modesty and decency in the new writings in favour of 'baring all' in the presentation of the sex act as reflected in Doreen Baingana's *Tropical Fish,* Kaine Agary's *Yellow-Yellow*, and Chimamanda Adichie's *Half of a Yellow Sun* risks misrepresenting the African experience. These writings move the issue of sex, which some older writers treat with cautious euphemism, into the open reflecting a 'modern' attitude towards the sexual. This reality, perhaps informs Charles Nnolim's (2006) assertion that members of the new generation of African writers are lacking a clear vision of the future and effective strategies to transform their societies.

Towards the Future

There is a need for a meaningful discourse on the future of African literature especially in articulating the anxiety of being in the twenty-first century. There is also the need to consider critical issues such as identity, language and social vision of African writers from multi-dimensional perspectives. Bearing in mind that African literary engagement involves creative writing and criticism, it is necessary to consider not only the creative output of Africans, but also to engage with the critical practice that drives the African literary tradition. Another crucial aspect is the nature of the teaching curriculum and research agenda in African literature in the universities. The critical foundation for a re-assessment of African literature should ordinarily begin with a review of the curriculum of the universities in Africa. This will enable new voices to be raised toward the re-invention of a new paradigm shift in African literature. The emergence of an all-inclusive African literature curriculum will enhance the drive towards African integration, which the African Union has found quite difficult to achieve.

In many higher institutions in Africa, the host department for the academic engagement of literary studies is usually the department of English, French or European languages, as the case may be. The teaching and learning of literature in European languages is being pursued without much consideration for the developments of literature produced in indigenous African languages. The current situation where African literature is learnt and taught in many universities in Africa as a 'minor appendage' to mainstream European literature needs to be re-considered. The notion of African literature as presently constructed is grossly tilted towards Western European literary canons and traditions, without due acknowledgement of the rich repertoire and development of literature in African languages. There is, therefore, an urgent need to discountenance the undue emphasis on European literatures in African universities and promote innovative 'difference' in their relationship to a pan-African literary heritage. The call for the 'decolonization of African literature' by Chinweizu and Ihechukwu (1988) deserves to be taken seriously. The predominant Eurocentric standards cannot adequately promote African interests in literary exegesis.

This proposition becomes inevitable because it points towards the future, and significantly resolves unanswered questions of several years. The abandonment of European languages for African languages, as suggested by Ngugi wa Thiong'o, may be counter-productive at this point, especially against the backdrop of the globalization wave sweeping across the world. The peculiarity of African experience can no longer be localized through writing in indigenous languages.

Being aware of the unstructured manner of the notion of globalization, Anthony Giddens has conceptualized it within the literary field as 'an intensification of global social interrelations by which distant localities are connected to one another' (in Grabovzki 2003:45). The translation of a plethora of works in African indigenous languages into European languages holds immense possibilities, which will grant greater access to them.

Even where a measure of free movement has been achieved, as seen in West Africa, the anglophone/francophone barrier erected by the colonialists constitutes a major impediment to the appreciation of literatures across the region. This necessitates a massive translation of African literatures written in Arabic, English, French, or Portuguese into other languages for accessibility within the African context. The provision of institutional support for such efforts by governmental and non-governmental organisations is crucial. More so, pan-Africanism, in the words of Abdul-Rahman, needs 'to leave the confines of conferences and mansions of our leaders to become part and parcel of our lives, building from below upwards' (2010:233). Greater cooperation needs to be fostered among the writers in Africa through exchange visits.

In addition, the study of oral literature needs to be intensified and moved into the centre of literary studies from its present marginal position. This also applies to the oral performances of diverse ethnic groups on the continent. They should form significant part of the syllabi in literary and performance studies. The impression that African literature is a single entity can be misleading, as there are hundreds of literatures even within nation states like Nigeria and South Africa. In considering the enormous diversity of literary experience in Africa, selected studies of the literatures written in African languages such as Amharic, Fulfulde, Hausa, Mande, Somali, Swahili, Xhosa, Zulu, Wolof, and Yoruba among other languges could form part of the core aspect of the literature. Literature is not all about printed texts; studying oral literature has shown that it has as much textuality as well as social and cultural importance. As Ruth Finnegan (2007:181) explains, there are great benefits in moving from a position where written texts seemed to hold central reality to the richness of oral expression and performance'.

The fact that Africa does not have a common African language should be a strength rather than weakness, as the study of these diverse literatures and their explicit comparativeness would promote better understanding and enhance integration among African people. A crucial aspect of the study of literature in African languages includes the literary history of such languages, the study of the early writers prior to the colonial period, African indigenous knowledge and folklore. It is possible for Africa to contribute significantly to global literary dialogue through this process. Beyond the consideration of early writers in African languages, studies in African literature should look beyond the confines of academic writings and take into account what Chinweizu (1988:xviii) refers to as 'those works which found, and have found, audiences outside the ivory tower'. In this category are works by the griots, minstrels, ballad singers, chanters and poets (*djelli, akewi*) who use indigenous languages to practise their arts.

A closely related matter is the urgent need to revisit the paradigms of critical practice and research. African literature must recapture and integrate the social theories of African intellectuals into its critical discourse. The dominance of literary theories inspired by Western epistemology should naturally give way to the profound articulation of the visions and thoughts of African thinkers and intellectuals such as Aimé Césaire, Amilcar Cabral, Ali Mazrui, Fatima Mermissi, Julius Nyerere, Kwame Nkrumah, Léopold Sédar Senghor, Nnamdi Azikwe, Obafemi Awolowo, Walter Rodney, Frantz Fanon, Tajudeen Abdul-Raheem, Wole Soyinka, Patrik Wilmot and Ngugi wa Thiong'o among others. As Hamdy Abdel Rahman (2010:177) argues, it is high time that Africa 'define its vision of future based on culture, existence and independence history'.

When Aimé Césaire, Leon Dumas and Léopold Sénghor came up with the idea of *négritude* in the 1930s, they readily captured the totality of the experience of colonized francophone Africa. They proffered intellectual answers to the dilemma of many Africans concerning French colonial assimilation policy. According to Senghor, 'négritude is neither racialism nor self negation; it is nothing more or less than what some English-speaking Africans have called the African personality...the "sum of the cultural values of the black world...it is a humanism of the twentieth century"' (1970:179–80). Through the recognition of the intellectual responses of African writers, African literature should give voice to the critical reflections on African living experience and developmental challenges. It should also influence how people respond to 'social and political order and the nature, desirability and direction of change' in Africa (Diamond 1985:435).

Conceived and valued as belonging to the past, oral texts are no longer automatically assumed to be a fixed unchanging heritage. There are several contemporary African verbal artists, young and old, in rural and urban settings, who have responded to change by incorporating innovative verbal elements in their artistic production or mediating their art through newer technologies such as radio, television, compact discs, all constituting the emergent oral texts. Here, there is a transmutation of the verbal form from the oral tradition to contemporary urban dynamics as expressed in popular culture. A specific illustration is how the traditional wrestling of Serer people in Senegal transits from its humble beginning to a thriving national popular culture, with multinational companies competing to sponsor the competition.

Beyond the economies of Senegalese traditional wrestling is the dynamism of African festive drama. A permanent feature of the wrestling context is the hybrid cultural phenomenon that combines the African traditional form with the Western. The musical accompaniment, the chants by the Senegalese women, the ritual performance of the wrestlers and the 'media war' during the wrestling competitions in Dakar, all add to the impression of the dynamism of African culture. Another example is David Coplan's (1995) study of how oral poetry of Zolani Mkiva on compact discs has been set to cotemporary hip pop music. The above examples are practical demonstrations of Fredrick's Jameson's (1991: 23) argument that 'popular culture is global rather than a national phenomenon'.

Conclusion

In the search for a viable path for the future of African literature, a well-crafted vision of the future and effective strategies to engender transformation are imperative. This raises the practical application of the digital space, the internet and related innovative technology as new paradigms of knowledge to African literary engagement. But the absence of a critical standard remains a bane of this development. The creation of a pan-African literature project is a matter of priority. As part of this effort, we should consider the establishment of a pan-African literary website, which could harness the trend of online publishing. Though there are existing online outlets, the idea is to have an authoritative outlet for the wide networks of scholars, writers, critics and other users from different parts of Africa. The growing momentum of online African writing can provide the tipping point for the future of African literature. The increase in the number of users with smart phones and the arrival of social media will 'further reinforce – in the minds of several writers – the idea that the future of African literature perhaps lies online' (Adenekan 2012:11).

The transitions from traditional print culture to an electronic 'hypertext project' is important. The strength of the hypertext is in its provision of links and access to information of various kinds, which users can browse at will (Berners-Lee and Cailliau 1993:1). Many of the books published by African writers are inaccessible to readers in different parts of Africa. This makes the provision of the electronic version of books imperative. Short stories, poems, performances and plays could also be posted on such a website for the consumption of the online public.

The appropriation of new media technology may have great consequences for teaching, learning and research in African literature. Texts may experience different processes of transformation through various creative engagements, making the creative piece to be unfixed and susceptible to changes. For many young African writers, new media technology offers a new avenue and an extraordinary platform to create, shape and re-shape fresh contemporary values. It signals an important way through which some of the emerging African voices negotiate the relationship between their works, themselves, Africa and their audience. Therefore, African writers, critics and scholars should begin to take advantage of the transition of texts across a multiplicity of media.

Just as the language of colonialism is being used to write back, the urgency of exploring new media technology for cyber-communication may promote African literary integration. Moreso, when it obviously offers immense possibilities for the future of African literature.

References

Abdul-Raheem, T., 2010, 'Taking Pan-Africanism to the People', in Biney, A. and A. Olukoshi, eds, *Speaking Truth to Power: Selected Pan African Postcards*. Dakar: Pambazuka.

Achebe, Chinua, 1975, *Morning Yet on Creation Day*, London: Heinemann.

Adenekan, O., 2012, 'African Literature in the Digital Age: Class and Sexual Politics', in 'New Writing from Nigeria and Kenya'. PhD thesis, Centre for West African Studies, University of Birmingham.

Adeoti, G. and Evwierhoma, M., 2006, *After the Nobel Prize: Reflections on African Literature, Governance, and Development.* Lagos: Association of Nigerian Authors.

Adepitan, T., 2006, 'New Fiction from Africa', in *African Literature Today 25*.

Afolayan, S., 2002, 'The Question of Postcolonial Culture: Language, Ideology and Cultural Essentialism', *Jouvert*, 7 (1): 1–11.

Appiah, K. A., 1992, *In My Father's House: Africa in the Philosophy of Culture*, Oxford: Oxford University Press.

Armah, A. K., 1968, *The Beautyful Ones are not Yet Born*, London: Heinemann.

Attree, L., ed., 2011, *To see the Mountain and Other Stories: The Caine Prize for African Writing*, Oxford: New Internationalist.

Berners-Lee, T. and Cailliau, 1993, 'The World Wide Web Initiative', Pro.C.Inet 1–10.

Booker, K., 1998, *The African Novel in English: An Introduction*, Portsmouth: Heinemann.

Chinweizu, Onwucheka J. and Ihechukwu M., 1988, *Toward the Decolonization of African Literature*, Enugu: Fourth Dimension.

Chinweizu, Onwucheka J., 1988, *Voices from* Twentieth *Century Africa: Griots and Town criers*, London: Faber & Faber.

Coplan, D., 2008, *In Township Tonight: South Africa Black Music and Theatre*, Chicago Chicago University Press.

Diamond, L., 1988, 'Fiction as Political Thought', *African Affairs*, 88(352): 435–45.

Diop, C. A., 1978, *The Cultural Unity of Black Africa*, Chicago: Third World.

Emenyonu, E.N., 2006, *New Directions in African Literature*, African Literature *Today 25* Oxford and Trenton, NY: James Currey and Africa World Press.

Emenyonu, E.N., 2006, 2010, *New Novels in African Literature Today 27*, Woodbridge: Jame Currey.

Emenyonu, E.N., 2006, *2011, Teaching African Literature Today*, Woodbridge: James Currey.
Finnegan, R., 2007, *The Oral Background and Beyond: Doing Things with Words in Africa*, Chicago: Chicago University Press.
Gimson, W., 1984, *Neuromancer*, New York: Beckley.
Grabovzki, E., 2003, 'The Impact of Globalization and the New Media on the notion of World Literature', in Zepenet, S. T., ed., *Comparative Literature and Comparative Cultural Studies*, Purdue: Purdue University Press.
Hale, T., 2006, 'Bursting at the Seams: New Dimensions for African Literature in the twenty-first Century', *African Literature Today 25*, 10–21.
Harrow, K., 1994, *Thresholds of Change in African Literature*, Portsmouth: Heinemann.
Hamilton, R., 2004, 'African Literature in Portuguese', in Abiola Irele and Simon Gikandi, eds, *The Cambridge History of African and Caribbean Literature 2*. Cambridge: Cambridge University Press.
Irele, A., 2001, *The African Imagination: Literature in Africa and the Black Diaspora*, Oxford: Oxford University Press.
Jameson, F., 1991, *Postmodernism or, The Cultural Logic of Late Capitalism*, Durham: Duke University Press.
Kunene, D., 1992, 'African-language Literature: Tragedy and Hope', *Research in African Literatures* 23(1), 7–15.
Lindfors, B., 2006, 'A Last Shot at the Twentieth Century Canon', *African Literature Today 25*.
Na'Allah, A., Garuba, H. and Esanwame, U., 2005, 'The Short Century After: African Literatures and Cultures from 1945–2005', *Canadian Review of Comparative Literature* 32 (3): 267.
Nnolim, C., 2006, 'African Literature in the twenty-first Century: Challenges for Writers and Critics', *African Literature Today 25*.
Olaniyan, T. and Quayson, A., 2007, *African Literature: An Anthology of Criticism and Theory*, Malden: Blackwell.
Osofisan, F., 2009, 'Wounded Eros and Cantillating Cupids: Sensuality and the Future of African Literature in Post-Military Era', in Eyisi, J., Odimegwu, I. and Ezenwa-Ohaeto, N., eds, *African literature and Development in the Twenty first Century: Proceedings of Ezenwa-Ohaeto International Memorial Conference*. Owerri: Living Flames Resources.
Senghor, L., 1970, 'Negritude: A Humanism of the Twentieth Century', in Kilson, M. and Cartey, W., *The African Reader: Independent Africa*, 179–92. New York: Random House.
wa Thiong'o., Ngugi, 1986, *Decolonizing the Mind: The Politics of Language in African Literature*, London: James Currey.
Wali, O., 1963, 'The Dead End of African Literature', *Transition* 10: 13–15.
Zeleza, P., 2007, 'Colonial Fictions: Memory and History in Yvonne Vera's Imagination', *Research in African Literatures* 38 (2): 9–21.

6

A Critical Analysis of Prophetic Myths in the Selected Fiction of Ben Okri

Olusola Ogunbayo

Introduction

In the search for a panacea to Africa's socio-political and economic malaise, scholars from various intellectual backgrounds, including literary critics, have offered perceptive solutions. For instance, critics have studied the writing of Ben Okri, the renowned Nigerian novelist, as a template. Mathew Green, in his study of *A Way of Being Free and Mental Fight* (Romanticism 2008), argues for an imaginative engagement with the economic base of history; while Mabiala Kenzo, also reading *The Famished Road*, opines that there should be a borrowing of 'insights from resources that are both endogenous and exogenous to Africa and their own tribal contexts' (2004:1) such that the travails occasioned by religious bigotry would be forestalled. From a literary perspective, Douglas McCabe (2005) and Esther de Bruijn (2007), in the context of *The Famished Road*, are in counter-dialogue of whether Africa's bankruptcy should be resolved with new ageism or cosmopolitanism. In fact, speculations about an ideal Africa in this century have become divergent and are increasingly becoming problematic themselves, exemplified by McCabe and Bruijin's stand-off, because there are no perfect solutions.

However, there seems to be an area which is yet to be given sufficient attention, even though it can also generate valuable insights into the source of Africa's predicament. This involves the use of myth as a predictive tool.

The term 'myth' has been variously defined by sociologists (Emile Durkheim, E.B Tylor), political theorists (Georges Sorel, Max Muller) and structuralists (Claude Lévi-Strauss) and African writers (Wole Soyinka, Isidore Okpewho).

However, what unites their views is the idea that a myth is a story. For the purpose of this study, a myth can be described as an imaginative account, animated by human and supernatural beings, which is projected towards explaining a phenomenon in life. The meaning-seeking tendency in humans enables them, at every moment of uncertainty and despair, to invent stories which tend to reveal the underlying patterns of things. A myth is invented through the imagination, the faculty that enables us to think of something that is not immediately present.

There are different kinds of myths. Broadly speaking, they can be classified into various categories such as cosmic myths, myths of gods, hero myths, religious myths, political myths, social myths, literary myths, philosophical myths and even scientific myths. Eliade contends that an account is mythic insofar as it 'reveals something as having been fully manifested and this manifestation is at the same time creative and exemplary since it is a foundation…of a kind of behaviour' (2004:18). This idea is corroborated by Eleazar Meletinsky who opines that 'Myths are a means of gaining insight into the human spirit' (2000: 56). The complexity of human behaviour is aptly captured in the indeterminate and unpredictable nature of literature. Myth presents plots and situations that are probable in human behaviour. An action or 'a kind of behaviour' can be foretold through the medium of myth since the primary function of myth is to explain and to describe. This correlates with Alan Watt's statement that 'Myth is to be defined as a complex of stories…which for various reasons, human beings regard as a demonstration of the inner meaning of the universe and of human life' (1953:7). The future is also a 'kind of behaviour' and it can be foretold through myth. The 'demonstration of the inner meaning' of the universe is expressed through the creation of myths. But when this demonstration' tends to explain 'a kind of behaviour' in the future, the myth can be described as a prophetic myth.

The explanatory function of a myth links it with prophecy which primarily means a prediction. Prophecy can also be described as the foreknowledge of future events. Prophecies can be in form of a message of warning, a return to a kind of behaviour, an advice to desist from an attitude, or an outright proclamation of impending doom. In this regard, there are social prediction, psychological prediction, religious prediction and political prediction. With the deployment of human and non-human characters, myth fashions themes, plots and situations which serve as analogy or imaginative representation of 'a kind of behaviour' in the future. This is what is meant by a myth explaining the future or predicting later occurrences.

That novelists and prophets have something in common is an idea with a long history. A cursory look at Western literary tradition, for example, reveals great poets such as Dante, Milton and Blake as having viewed themselves and presented themselves to the world in one way or the other as endowed with prophetic gift or divinely inspired speech. However, these writers inherited earlier traditions of literature as prophecy, evident through the Middle Ages in Christian Europe and Muslim Spain and the East and ancient Greece. For instance, pilgrims from beyond the Greek city-states flocked to major oracles, especially at Delphi, to ask for divine advice about marriage, children, money matters, and even foreign policy. The responses were always in riddles, poetry, verses, images, symbols and esoteric expressions because gods were too complex to reply clearly to mere human beings. These narratives of the gods were often animated by imaginative characters like the Olympian gods who emblematise certain realistic happenings

In deploying myth as prophecy, Okri, in *Astonishing the Gods* (1995) *and In Arcadia* (2002), takes recurring patterns of the human imagination and repetitive historical happenings to form archetypal templates that foreshadow the future. This artistic style aligns with Lévi-Strauss's structural delineation of myth as a diachronic narrative that records the historical past and a synchronic means of explaining the present and even the future. Okri's artistic construct is to show the cause-and-effect of recurring archetypes and to suggest preventive approaches which can forestall human socio-political and economic disasters. For instance, in *In Arcadia*, Okri presents universal archetypal themes and experiences such as quest, journey, betrayal, adventure, pain and reward, all forming a plot that can be read as showing the things to come as they apply to Africa and the global context. Whereas in *Astonishing the Gods*, history is mythologised in a way that the texts reveal their rootedness in material happenings, with a view to underlining the contradictions of the future. In view of this, the mythic imagination serves as a vehicle for understanding trends and current affairs because the current degeneration of reality is a function of somebody's imaginative making. Dictatorship, for instance, is a myth conceived by an inhuman, insensitive government, just like terrorism and kidnapping are the mythical constructs of religious fundamentalists. Against this backdrop, it is our contention that a myth can be a means of understanding another myth. Apart from this, it can be used to anticipate and predict the consequences of a current, acceptable myth.

Nonetheless, in the course of mythologising the ideal pattern for the future, Okri, through mythmaking, also re-invents the image of Africa as a continent of hope, progress and creativity. This supports Simon Gikandi's view in 'Foreword: On Afropolitanism' that Africans should tell their stories not only to address their local travails, but also to 'respond to transnational challenges, of the complicated relationships between regions and traditions within Africa, and…in building cultural bridges between countries, language and localities' (2011:11).

In the light of the destruction of lives and human values in Africa, the potential of the mythical imagination to foresee certain events should be considered as an integral factor in corporate development. In support of Georges Sorel's *Reflections* (1961) and Wole Soyinka's *Myth, Literature and the African World* (1976), which set out their positions on the pragmatic nature of myth, this essay argues that with mythic imagination and the ability to decipher recurring patterns in the march of history, Africans can come to recognise the universal in any set of material circumstances. It is then that the people can anticipate the danger of Western 'generosity'. It is then that we can spot the making of a dictator and, of course, it is then that we can foresee dearth and starvation borne out of an archetypal pattern of waste and instant gratification.

Okri's concern for Africa's condition in *In Arcadia* is articulated through Lao, Okri's persona and official narrator, who introduces readers to the archetypal characters involved in the odyssey to Arcadia. Critics like Violetta Verge (2004: 4), have argued that Lao is an African, since his traits align with a socio-religious peculiarity of Africans. Lao envisions Okri's myth of the search of lost origin, where the past is revisited, understood and deconstructed in order to project into the future. Arcadia, in this discussion, is the mythical explanation of what the individual or corporate Africa is seeking: Arcadia is serenity occasioned by sensitive, democratic governance; it is the dependable justice system and the security of lives and property. Arcadia is also the place where Africans can sleep with their eyes closed. Arcadia is the picture, 'the desire that each human being cherishes in this short journey called life' (Verge 2004:6). Okri, through Lao, mythologises the future of Africa through the symbol of Arcadia.

Similarly, in *Astonishing the Gods*, Okri engages the concept of change achieved through the mythical explanation of the future. For Okri, the future can be anticipated and understood when individuals, or the corporate entity called Africa, decide to liberate (what he polemically means by 'astonish') themselves from the false consciousness and the mental inhibition imposed by the ruling mythmakers of our time (the gods). These gods are inhumane power brokers, selfish business moguls who have enormous influence on the economic base. These gods would only be astonished if their myths (laws, trends, policies) are understood, anticipated, and checked before they become the ideologies of the time. Myth is the language of change and the tool for the astonishment of the gods. Both *Astonishing the Gods* and *In Arcadia* are about the use of the mythic imagination to understand trends, to know the antecedents thereof, and to symbolically suggest the likelihood of certain events to recur. To do these, Okri deploys a strong universal archetype called the journey in both texts. The journey or quest archetype is akin to Africa's tortuous odyssey through the labyrinths of hunger, war, dictatorship, inequality, and general pessimism.

Journey as Archetypal Motif

In the exploration of the journey motif in his works, Okri has been influenced by African thought. For instance, he is aware of 'Abiku' metaphysics (birth and rebirth journey) in the works of Wole Soyinka and J. P. Clark; also of Western mythical models like Daniel Defoe (2001, *Robinson Crusoe*), Jonathan Swift (2003, *Gulliver's Travels*), Thomas More (Utopia, 1516), and Francis Bacon (*New*

Atlantis, 1626), who have mythologised the idea of journey to suggest universal themes.

The journey archetype is about the hero in search of some truth to restore order and harmony to the land. It often includes the series of trials and tribulations that the hero faces along the way. Usually, the hero descends into a real or psychological hell and is forced to discover certain truths. Though the journey motif manifests itself in various ways, Okri's interest is in the journey archetype of transformation and change. Otherwise known as the archetypes of metamorphosis, the quest for transformation and change personifies the process of seeking out new options; tearing down what is no longer useful; committing to people, values and activities; and creating new forms.

The utilitarian value of the journey archetype is shown in transitional periods in individual lives (adolescence, midlife, retirement) as well as in corporate organisations (management reshuffles, change of policy statements, recruitment and so on). For the perennial issues in Africa, the journey archetype is apt in capturing lost values such as discipline, collectivity, respect, communality and hard work. To achieve this, Okri shows that individuals must leave the known to discover and explore the unknown. To save Africa in the 21st century, the individual must overcome loneliness and isolation, and seek out new paths. Thus, the journey archetype is unconventional and unorthodox, but it helps to open up new vistas to possibilities of a new life.

The journey archetype connects with the idea of prophecy because it suggests a connection with the past and a movement into the future. Like a prophecy, a traveller looks ahead and moves ahead. A journey involves a search; prophecy looks for what is in the future. A journey intends to solve a riddle by looking for a solution; prophecy seeks to answer the now by looking at the hereafter. To be successful, the quest for change and transformation must derive its strength from understanding, anticipating, and knowing recurring patterns of the past and present in order to guarantee a safe future. For Africa, the 21st century will only be a repetition of failures of the preceding one if, in the quest for change, the continent fails to spot inhibitions, inhumanity and dream-killers.

In Search of the Future: Mythical Paradigms as Prophecy in *In Arcadia*

The predicament of loss in individual and corporate contexts is the crux of *In Arcadia*. Early in the text, Okri announces the state of the nation and the tragedy of every individual as he bemoans: 'We had all lost something, and lost it a long time ago and didn't stand any chance of finding it again. We lost it somewhere before childhood began. Maybe our parents lost it for us, maybe we never had it…' (*In Arcadia*, p. 6). The loss in this narrative is defined as 'treasures hidden in Arcadia' (p. 5). By critical inference, these 'hidden treasures' refer to the future because the author hints that Arcadia denotes a place of tranquility. It is a place of panacea that must be arrived at by following the instructions of certain archetypal patterns (inscriptions/ messages) and characters (Malasso). Arcadia is a lost innocence, a missing factor, a blueprint for progress, a master key for the recovery of purpose and vision. There is a dimension of paradox to this as the future is what is missing in the past. In the context of Africa's socio-political predicament, the future means a loss of cultural values such as discipline, creativity, tolerance, forbearance, equity, and what Okri calls 'a refuge from the corrupting cities' (p. 65).

Arcadia is not a place: it is an act, a system. When this system is followed, then the bliss in Arcadia will naturally follow. Though the persona laments that he 'didn't feel that we could ever find it again' (p. 6), the mythical pattern of finding what is lost through the archetype of journey is immediately set in motion as the narrator begins to chart the way for journey into Arcadia, the future. Hence, the story begins as certain disillusioned archetypal characters (Lao, Propr, Dane, Sam, Jute, Husk, Riley) are set on a journey of instructions to Arcadia, the place in their future where, at least, 'to get away from our miserable attempts at propping up falling lives, away from the dehydrating boredom of the daily round in this inferno that we call the modern world' (p. 5), is a place of meaning. In Okri's mythology, this mythical pattern of journey carries with it other archetypes which help to reinforce the pursuit of Arcadia. They are the Oneness Archetype, Void Archetype and Nostalgia Archetype.

The first motivating archetype, which whets the appetite for the future, is the Oneness Archetype. This vision of Arcadia is portrayed in 'Book Two: Initiation in the Garden' where, like Biblical Garden of Eden, everything is the same 'woven in the cloth of mystery' (p. 42). There is no consciousness of good and evil, since nothing is labelled in binary opposites. This archetype is symbolic of a material condition where the world is free from tribalism, religious sectionalism, racism and ethnic rivalry. Though this may not be plausible in a quotidian sense, the pursuit of an Arcadian myth of Oneness is a step to progress. What drives the travellers into the pursuit of Arcadia is the enormity of division in the modern world where the Oneness Archetype is far-fetched, where everything is 'in broken pits' (p. 5). The insistence on names, partitioning and divisionary tactics often lead to the pollution and consequent loss of Arcadia. The challenge ahead of the travellers is to see that every human being is connected to another, just like the vegetation, forestry, tapestry and symmetry of Arcadia. Hence, Lao's de-humanising description of the co-travellers is technically and mythically corrected by the aesthetics of order, respect and oneness when the character comes to a self-realisation through the re-birth of the mind. Lao, at the beginning of the odyssey, cynically dismisses members of the filming crew as 'engenderers of chaos...interesting specimens of stressed humanity' (p. 63). However, after experiencing transformation at the sight of Arcadia, he declares: 'Living ough to be the unfolding masterpiece of the loving spirit' (p. 230). What Lao evolve from is the un-Arcadian attitude of setting boundaries, which naturally inhibit cross-cultural exchanges, knowledge acquisition and corporate growth. Using the Oneness Archetype, therefore, Okri foresees a possibility of change in the future, if humanity embraces what will guarantee that future: the myth of seeing things in a comprehensive, all-inclusive fashion.

Another handmaiden of the journey motif is the Void Archetype. Void in mythical epistemology signifies stillness. Void is akin to the yoga practice of meditation. Void is not mysticism but a human character of self-discipline which involves separation from distraction. It is a condition which fosters inspiration and philosophical moorings because it is a conscious attempt to avoid noise, the very undoing of postmodernism. 'In Book Three: Intuitions in the Dark' starts with noise: Lao, Sam, Husk, Riley Jute and Propr (a name suggestive of 'malapropism') are at the centre of pandemonium and perplexity which the author aptly captures as the spectacle of 'our receding soul' (p. 64).

Husk and Riley are busy giving significance to the show of turmoil by taking pictures of all the events. This anarchic fiesta of bedlam is deliberately set as a mythical binary opposite to the inspiring silence of Arcadia. Hence, an antidote to noise making, the opposing reality to the reign of disorderliness is created. From the character of Arcadia, Okri describes the Void Archetype as a progressive humanist act where 'The vistas of the world disappear, and the world surrenders to an omnipotent darkness… The mind contracts. The spirit folds inward. An open sky gives way to a closed world' (p. 67) because the 'tunnel', Okri's artistic term for the Void Archetype, 'makes us see inward, against our will' (p. 69). The value of the Void Archetype or stillness in the journey towards the future is that revelations, self-criticism and comprehensive awareness are impossible where everybody seeks for attention and where significance is given to outward shows of carnality, improprieties, and vulgarism as exemplified by the ingloriousness of Jute and Sam especially. The Void factor demands separatism, objective clarification, impersonality where one can see 'strong sunlight and strong shadow' and perceive the values of their complementarities. Void also implies 'darkness', but it also mean that things, ideas and people that are regarded as unwanted, unconventional, and are often wasted and neglected have immense values.

The journey archetype as a tool for prediction also carries with it the Nostalgia Archetype. In Okri's mythical construct, the Nostalgia Archetype captures the travellers' longing and yearning for transformation. Nostalgia as an archetype means a desire to return to a former time in one's life or a sentimental yearning for the happiness of a former place or time. The Nostalgia Archetype is noticeable in Lao's remark at the beginning that 'We had all lost something…' (p. 6). Though they are all sucked into a seemingly irredeemable quagmire, each character in *In Arcadia* nurses cherished dreams for Arcadia, the future.

In 'Book Five', the nostalgic feelings of each of them carry peculiar labels such as 'Jim's Nightmare', 'Mistletoe's Dream' and 'Riley's Regret', and so on. Each designation denotes the missing dream and the lost vision of each character. The intent of this mythic device is to create a thirst for the future, where the characters long for fulfillment. In 'Jim's Intuition', for instance, lies Okri's concern for the activation of mental potentials as well as the cultivation of natural resources. He foresees a situation in the future where inactivity and indolence can, again, lead to a loss, thus rendering the Arcadia destination far-fetched:

> Immensity of the land
> And spaces of the sun.
> They slept too long in paradise
> And ended up in prison. (p. 178)

Jim has stayed too long being idle. According to Lao, he is 'squat and fat and balding' and he 'Hadn't directed anything in at least seven years… Incompetent beyond description' (p. 10). Jim needs the Arcadian project to get back to his feet; he knows that there is something he has lost. The African continent is bedeviled with Jims who are the directors of dreams and corporate visions. They are the parliamentarians who cannot enact a profitable law because they have failed to utilise the 'Immensity of the land'. There are individual Jims also. There are 'spaces', and ideas that are yet to be cultivated in the community because of indolence. In Jim's intuition, Okri projects the consequence of following a pattern of idleness: 'prison'.

Jute, the puritan and spy, suffers a character deformity which makes her long for a future where she will no more be seen as 'the intolerant…the echoing corridors of dreadful institutions' (p. 15). From her intuition of Arcadia, she sees the future implication of sternness, wanton callousness and institutionalised calumny, which are her key attributes. Jute is symbolic of organised religion, motivated by the selfish doctrines of charlatanism, bigotry and extremism. She knows what she has lost as the images of Arcadia warn her of the implication of her insensitivity and fastidiousness. Every overly critical officialdom and suspecting policing institutions have hidden contradictions such as hypocrisy, high-profile secrets and hidden agendas. Hence, they read their fears in other peoples' affairs. But Jute foresees that '…tyrants and dictators all had their Arcadias to cleanse their souls of the brutalities they had unleashed' because puritanical expectations have implications on the Jutes of this world. But shouldn't organised institutions have laws, monitoring officers and principles? Yes, but every Jute archetype must have an Arcadian human-face where 'There are an affront to a world reeking with suffering and starvation'. This is what Jute has lost; hence, the nostalgia.

Popr is nostalgic for the times people used to listen to him, but he lost on the grounds of his indifference to people's voices. He loves to make sound (meanings, statements, ideational remarks) but he is 'tone deaf' to other people's points of view because he spends his time 'listening to garbage' (p. 11). He is thus, reaping what he has sown. Propr has lost his audienceship: he is a player without spectators. On his way to Arcadia, he longs for that missing link in his sound-making career: how to carry people along, how to project, how to be democratic. On a larger scale, he is a leader without followers. Arcadia, to him, is a picturesque of the values inherent in listening by not ignoring 'the cries of the people' (p. 178). Here, Okri, in conjunction with the universal law of Karma, uses the Nostalgic Archetype to foresee the future of a non-listening leader as exemplified by Prop's nostalgia.

The readers can have a glimpse of the future from Okri's narratives because the characters, accompanied with 'fears…failures, the problems that had haunted their fathers' (p. 6), are on a tortuous journey. Okri affirms that 'all the possibilities of our lives run parallel to one another' (Palmer 2002). Through the foregoing archetypes, he warns of the dangers of repeating the miasmic attitudes so that the bliss of Arcadia can be experienced. Arcadia is in the mind: it is not a place that can be reached physically. It is only attained through the process of evolving and constant re-birth.

Unorthodox Archetypes as Predictive Myth

Like *In Arcadia*, Okri's *Astonishing the Gods* continues the probing of reality through the journey archetype. But unlike *In Arcadia*, the narratives revolve around a nameless character who embarks on a quest that leads to the island of the Invisibles. Following the instruction of invisible guides (a man, a child and a woman), he roams through strange terrains and hallucinatory landscapes. Later, he finds a bridge that is characterised by myth, magic, ideas and dreams. Crossing it, he leaps into an ethereal land, a potentially utopian city. This plot structure is reminiscent of D. O. Fagunwa's *Ogboju Ode Ninu Igbo Irunmale* (1983, translated by Wole Soyinka as *The Forest of a Thousand Daemons*). The point of departure is that *Astonishing* the Gods is about humankind's discovery of personal and institutional flaws. While Fagunwa's novel is preoccupied with the themes of will, survival, tenacity and determination, *Astonishing* the Gods is about the unearthing of individual and corporate potentials in order to challenge a reigning ideology or to 'astonish' 'the gods' of this world.

'Astonish' in 'astonishing the gods' connotes assessing, anticipating, predicting, challenging and thereby subverting the ways of inhumane establishments in order to counter their narrative. The 'gods' means those who hold the reins of power, not necessarily a divine being. In order to astonish the gods, each individual must embark on a personal quest (it is a collective quest in *In Arcadia*, though the characters receive an individual intuition) to probe the future of those who impose pain and difficulty. This narrative, therefore, is about change. The change is to challenge a current ideological process which has attributed universality to certain issues that are highly contingent. The anonymous hero of *Astonishing the Gods* seeks to challenge the hegemonic structure of institutionalised inequity by searching for alternative patterns of thought. This change is necessitated by the use of language to paint a desired future. In searching for an alternative episteme, Okri stretches and strengthens the journey archetype with the use of the Unorthodox Archetypal Statement and Unorthodox Archetypal Sight.

Unusual expressions are stated in a way that challenges readers to ponder for a while before they begin to identify with them. The meaning of these strange statements by Okri unfolds in the course of the narrative. The seemingly weird expressions lead the reader on like a guide into the future; to the end of the book. These unconventional remarks encourage the readers to share in the burden of the nameless character because there is an unconscious connection with what they mean. They are strange but familiar. They are statements that are missing in religious books, constitutions, policies, publications, educational curricula, myths and folklores. They are not there because the ruling ideas have expunged them, leaving the credos of hypocrisy and instant gratification to thrive. While these strange statements can be regarded as 'paradoxes', they are referred to in this essay as 'Unorthodox Archetypal Statements' because they remind the readers of deep rooted truths, goading their imaginations to reflect on the things to come.

In another sense, Okri presents novel insights that cast a *déjà vu* feeling on the traveller/readers. These seemingly strange sights are not really strange because they appear as if they have been seen somewhere before. Though the visual elements presented are different from the pollution of the material world, the traveller can identify with them, because they are the ideals that he longs for. These sights are graphic images which generate the intuitions and recognition of what is to come. Unorthodox Archetypal Sights are used as prophecy because they are presented as desired visions of what can result from the disturbing values of the ruling establishment and what means exist in astonishing, subverting and counteracting the self-imposing 'gods'. In an actual sense, the traveller has lost his identity and visibility because his education, fashioned according to the curriculum of human imperialists, does not teach him that he exists. Hence, his search is to look for visibility, for meaning.

> It was in books that he first learnt of his invisibility.
> he searched for himself and his people in all the history books
> he read and discovered to his youthful astonishment that
> he didn't exist. This troubled him so much that he resolved,
> as soon as he was old, to leave his land and find the people
> who did exist, to see what they looked like. (*Astonishing the Gods*, p. 3)

From the excerpt above, it is clear that this character has been robbed of his 'being'. He is so psychologically retarded that he does not see himself.

Unorthodox Archetypal Statements

The following are archetypal statements worthy of further consideration: 'You are seeking something that you have already found, but you don't know it.' This statement is made by 'a gentle voice' (p. 6) to the traveller after seven years. The second is: 'You must master the art of happiness' (p. 9). Another is: 'Retain your bewilderment. Your bewilderment will serve you well' (p. 11). Others are: 'Understanding leads to ignorance, especially, when it comes too soon' (p. 30); 'When you make sense of something, it tends to disappear. It is only mystery which keeps things alive' (p. 30); 'Too much beauty is bad for the soul...want some ugliness...some suffering' (p. 77); 'Things loose their reality if you are not aware of them' (p. 104). These statements encapsulate Okri's mythic idea of prediction.

From the foregoing, it is clear that Okri, through the traveller's travail and the guiding statements he receives, is disenchanted with current protocols. The statements, paradoxical in nature, are geared towards encouraging the readers to remember some primordial ideas that materialism and carnality have made them forget. These words reawaken patterns of wisdom that humankind share but have not remembered. They provide insights into how the future can be better. Individuals and corporate entities (Africa for example) seek aids, loans and assistance that are not necessary because they have, in abundance, material and human resources needed for progress. But the places where these potentials are kept can no longer be remembered. Other things, such as oil bunkering, political maneuvering, election rigging and power struggle, have replaced creative memory with amnesia. To guarantee a better future, the continent must take cognisance of the archetypal statement of looking for the missing future inside the region rather than begging. This is also a way of mastering 'the art of happiness'. Happiness and corporate well-being are experiences that must be prepared for. Tranquility does not come on a gold plate. By finding lost resources from the inside, the happiness of the future is secured.

Okri, with the archetype of 'Bewilderment', foresees a future guaranteed by the sustained character of curiosity, wonder and search, all connotative of research. There is no progress without research. It is inimical to growth if the funds allocated to instant gratification, materialism and largesse are greater than the time and resources devoted to research in health and education. 'Bewilderment' is an asset, because it imbues in humans, the progressive temper of curiosity. Therefore, to pretend that there is much 'understanding' is the greatest inhibition to postmodern development. The claim to full wisdom on the grounds of pomposity and self-aggrandisement is a threat to the future because it is 'only mystery which keeps things alive'. A person or society that has lost the sense of 'bewilderment' (research) and 'mystery' (myth) has lost the future.

Unorthodox Archetypal Sights

The signs and symbols of governing institutions are ideologically marked. These ideas are subtly motivated by greed, avarice, carnality and personal aggrandisement. Over the years, elite institutions have semiotically manifested the ideology of selfishness, power, drunkenness, and financial recklessness especially in terms of governance. Unfortunately, these inhumane images seem to be gaining equal stature with truth because the governing myth has become the language used to impose interpretative structure on the psyche of the people. Through signs and symbols, therefore, Okri deploys mythical images that challenge the inhumane motifs of the ruling signs by predicting the contradictions which come with following them.

As the traveller passes through the verandah of the Invisible City, Okri gives a description which evokes the vision of order, reminiscent of John's portrayal of the New Jerusalem in the Book of Revelation: 'Lost in wonder, he stared at the white harmonic buildings round the square. He noticed their pure angels, their angelic buttresses, and their columns of gleaming marble...He noticed how all things invisible seemed to become attentive to the glorious singing which poured a glow into the limpid moonlight' (p. 7). If there is any anomaly with which the ruling ideology is fraught, it is disorderliness. In Okri's mythic view, therefore, the future can be saved from the atrocities of the 'divide and rule' tacticians, if only there is a strong sense of socio-political harmony and institutional coherence. Differences must be understood while an individual part is 'attentive to the glorious singing' of other parts. This archetypal sight of harmony is apt in capturing Okri's perspective of how the future is likely to be if orderliness and coherence are stressed.

Apart from physical buildings that are visible, everything else in the island is described as invisible. In his paradoxical style, Okri portrays how futile it is, to be looking for visibility. This is demonstrated in books three and four. Visibility in this context means the quest for validation, acceptance and society's confirmation; it is the orthodox endorsement of what is normal, beautiful and laudable. There is much sadness and disillusionment in aspiring for societal acceptance through the medium of their constructed signs and symbols. The seeking of visibility is a sign of weakness, imitation and parody. Everyone needs original vision and visibility. The more invisible an individual or corporate society is, the more progressive, because to be visible is to follow the status quo of depravity and insensitivity which define the oppressors' visibilities.

The archetypal sight of nothingness or invisibility inspires the quest for growth and meaning-making. Those who set up disturbing appearances have done so to project their mythic conviction which is borne out of greed and wanton calumny. No wonder William Blake (cited in Marsh: 2001:88) avers that 'I must create a system or be enslaved by another man's'. To be safe and to guarantee a future worth living, individuals must form their visibilities. In *Astonishing the Gods*, the readers are taken through the travails and tragedies of those who seek for visibility. Okri presents an overdressed lady in her odyssey to the Invisible City. The traveller inquires where she is going and she replies 'I am going to where I can see people and where people can see me' (p. 77). But the traveller observes that the more she craves for visibility, the more she disappears: 'Just before she vanished into the temple, he thought he saw her smile. It occurred to him that ...she too was a paradox' (p. 78). In order to avoid a future of contradiction, one must not seek societal acceptance or what Okri connotes as visibility.

Conclusion

In the foregoing analysis, the journey archetype has been delineated as a mythic device used by Okri to construct the image of the lost ideal as it applies to the future. Actually, Arcadia is not a place that humankind can reach because it represents an 'idyll' future. But since the 'idyll' cannot be attained in actuality, the quest for Arcadia is an impulse to strive towards perfection, orderliness, harmony and corporate beauty. The future is always renewed by the unending visitation, research and reinterpretation of lost ideals. This requires personal sacrifice and self-criticism. The messages, inscriptions and intuitions given to each character in *In Arcadia* are to inspire them to rectify their individual anomalies in the light of what they want their future to be. Arcadia is an aesthetic vision meant to ameliorate individual and mass disillusionment of humankind.

From Okri's mythological stance, the change required in the future must start from the sacrifice of every individual. Self-sacrifice remains a timeless panacea for an ailing society. That is why Okri, in Astonishing the Gods, uses a single character to paint a future where each individual would be responsible for his destiny. We need not wait for government policies and democratic ideals to shape the future for us: we can individually predict what is to come and, if need be, change it for positive result. Sacrifice entails the consciousness of the voice of conscience, the practice of selflessness, the love of creativity, the use of perception and the engagement of self-reflection which are all characteristics of the mythical art of prediction.

However, are all these elements in *In Arcadia* and *Astonishing the Gods* prescriptive enough to redeem the suffering continent of Africa? Is the myth of prediction capable of liberating the African continent from the shackles of neo-colonialism, corruption and oppression? Are Okri's 'pictures' not 'sophisticated and unsettling' as Green observes? Okri's prophetic myths of Africa and the world may appear descriptive in the narratives, but these visions of 'Arcadia' and 'Invisible City' are artistic prescriptions which suggest the invaluable rewards of the discernment of causes through the observation of recurring pattern either in the past or the present. The utilitarian value of this artistic or psychic attitude is to prevent such undesirable features recurring in the desired future. The gods that create hunger, dearth, dictatorship, kidnapping and terrorism in Africa would be astonished if individuals and corporate bodies can learn how to predict their next lines of action. How would kidnapping succeed if the movements, hideouts and networks of the perpetrators can be predicted? What success awaits a terrorist for whom the timing of his bomb is stale news to law enforcement agents? An ideal Africa of the 21st century is possible if the lost purity, decency and orderliness which represent 'the first foundation of the golden age' (Astonishing the Gods, p. 130) can be mythically deciphered, embraced and utilised. This will not only tackle the problems of tyranny and violence, but also contribute to universal efforts to ensure the preservation of the human species.

References

Bacon, F., 1909–14 [1526], *The New Atlantis.* Vol. III, Part 2, The Harvard Classics, New York: P.F. Collier & Son.

de Bruijn, Esther, 2007, 'Coming to Terms with New Ageist Contamination: Cosmopolitanism in Ben Okri's *The Famished Road*', *Research in African Literatures* 38 (4): 170–86.

Defoe, Daniel, 2001, Robinson Crusoe [Reprint], New York: Aladdin Paperbacks.

Eliade, Mircea, 1967, *From Primitives to Zen: A Sourcebook of the History of Religions*, San Francisco: Harper and Row.

Flood, Christopher, 2002, *Political Myth: A Theoretical Introduction*, New York: Routledge.

Fraser, Robert, 2002, *Ben Okri*, United Kingdom: Northcote House Publisher.

Gikandi, Simon, 2011, 'Foreword: On Afroplitanism', in Jennifer Wawrzinek and J.K.S Makokha, eds, *Negotiating Afroplitanism: Essays on Borders and Spaces in Contemporary African Literature and Folklore*, New York: Rodop.

Green, Mathew, 2008, 'Dreams of Freedom: Magical Realism and Visionary Materialism in Okri and Blake', *Romanticism*. London: Edinburgh University Press.

Kenzo, Mabiala, 2004, 'Religion, Hybridity, and the Construction of Reality in Postcolonial Africa', in *Koninklijke*, Leiden: Brill.

McCabe, Douglas, 2005, '"Higher Realities": New Spirituality in Ben Okri's *The Famished Road', Research in African Literatures* 36 (4): 1–21.

Marsh, Nicholas, 2001, *William Blake: The Poems*, New York: Palmgrave

Meletinsky, Eleazar, 2000, *The Poetics of Myth*, London: Routledge.

More, T.,1989 [1516], *Utopia*, George M. Logan and Robert M. Adams, eds, Cambridge: Cambridge University Press.

Okri, Ben, 1981, *The Landscapes Within*, Longman: Harlow.

Okri, Ben, 1992, *The Famished Road*, Anchor: London.

Okri, Ben, 1993, Songs *of Enchantment*, London: Vintage.

Okri, Ben, 1995, .*Astonishing the Gods*, London: Phoenix House

Okri, Ben, 1996, *Dangerous Love*, London: Phoenix House.
Okri, Ben, 1998, *A Way of Being Free*, London: Phoenix House.
Okri, Ben, 1998, *Infinite Riches*, London: Phoenix House.
Okri, Ben, 1999, *Mental Fight*, London: Phoenix House.
Okri, Ben, 2002, *In Arcadia*, London: Phoenix House.
Sorel, Georges, 1961, *Reflections on Violence*, Collier Books: New York.
Soyinka, Wole, 1976, *Myth, Literature and the African World*, Cambridge: Cambridge University Press.
Soyinka, Wole, 1983, *The Forest of a Thousand Demons: A Hunter's Saga* (translation of D. O. Fagunwa's *Ogboju Ode Ninu Igbo Irunmale*), London: Random House.
Swift, Jonathan, 2003, *Gulliver's Travels*, Penguin Books: London.
Watts, Alan, 1953, *Myth and Ritual in Christianity*, Beacon Press: London.

Printed in the United States
By Bookmasters